I WANT TO SEE

Roc O'Connor, SJ

I WANT TO SEE

What the Story of Blind Bartimaeus Teaches Us about Fear, Surrender and Walking the Path to Joy

twentythirdpublications.com

TWENTY-THIRD PUBLICATIONS
One Montauk Avenue, Suite 200
New London, CT 06320
(860) 437-3012 or (800) 321-0411
www.twentythirdpublications.com

Copyright ©2017 Roc O'Connor, SJ. All rights reserved. No part of this publication may be reproduced in any manner without prior written permission of the publisher. Write to the Permissions Editor.

Scripture quotations are from *New Revised Standard Version Bible: Catholic Edition*, copyright © 1989, 1993 National Council of the Churches of Christ in the United States of America. Used by permission. All rights reserved worldwide.

Italics in quotations have been added for emphasis.

ISBN: 978-1-62785-327-9
Library of Congress Control Number: 2017953856
Printed in the U.S.A.

 A Division of Bayard, Inc.

Acknowledgments

For
Gerry Stockhausen, SJ
(1949–2016),
friend and classmate,
whose death set me next to Bartimaeus.
A blessing to so many in this life,
his dying has become a gift hidden
in secret places.

Thank you, Dan Connors
at Twenty-Third Publications.
And to Trish Sullivan Vanni
for being such a skillful midwife
to this manuscript.

I am grateful to so many mentors in my life,
especially those gifted with spiritual and
psychological insight. I thank the following:
John B. Foley, SJ; Larry Gillick, SJ; Bill Fulco, SJ;
Donald Bonnington, MD; Frank Burke, SJ;
Patrick Dougherty, LP; and Hal Dessel, LCSW.
I am also indebted to several others
who wished to remain incognito: Stephanie M.;
Mike P.; Patty C.; Jim S.; Marge O.; Jalinda R.;
Bill, Bob, and Dennis W.; and Tony R.

Contents

The Healing of the Blind Beggar   xi

Introduction   1

CHAPTER ONE
Blind by the Way   8

CHAPTER TWO
Which Way?   24

CHAPTER THREE
Blind Beggar by the Way   39

CHAPTER FOUR
Blind Disciples—Which Way?   52

CHAPTER FIVE
The Way toward Death—
Scribes and Pharisees   67

CHAPTER SIX
Five Infirm on the Way   85

EPILOGUE
Good News for the Way   100

I will give you the treasures

of darkness and riches hidden in secret

places, so that you may know that it is I,

the L<small>ORD</small>, *the God of Israel,*

who call you by your name.

ISAIAH 45:3

The Healing of the Blind Beggar

(Mark 10:46–52)

They came to Jericho. As he and his disciples and a large crowd were leaving Jericho, Bartimaeus son of Timaeus, a blind beggar, was sitting by the roadside. When he heard that it was Jesus of Nazareth, he began to shout out and say, "Jesus, Son of David, have mercy on me!" Many sternly ordered him to be quiet, but he cried out even more loudly, "Son of David, have mercy on me!" Jesus stood still and said, "Call him here." And they called the blind man, saying to him, "Take heart; get up, he is calling you." So throwing off his cloak, he sprang up and came to Jesus. Then Jesus said to him, "What do you want me to do for you?" The blind man said to him, "My teacher, let me see again." Jesus said to him, "Go; your faith has made you well." Immediately he regained his sight and followed him on the way.

Introduction

This is not the best way to start a book. In fact, it's a helluva way to start a book.

The two-year run-up to the election of 2016 revealed new depths of the festering divisions among citizens of the United States. It also exposed the ways many of us seek relief from our vulnerabilities. Feel weak? Blame someone! Feel impotent? Bully another! Feel small? Rage at others! Feel threatened? Escalate! Call them names. Intensify the savage drama. Target others to avoid feeling powerless. Kill 'em. Repeat.

There's a telling adage: *Hurt people hurt people.* Certainly since 9/11, we Americans have experienced levels of vulnerability, even impotence, in the face of terrorist attacks at home and abroad. The very dread we had held at bay for decades invaded our awareness and provoked pageants of power and pedantry that continue to prove themselves insufficient for alleviating our fears. We rely on our nation's might to ward off the very angst that plagues us, yet there aren't enough distractions or bluster to return us to the peace of mind of summer 2001.

We have turned our righteous indignation toward our enemies—or against the most vulnerable—to relieve our shame. As we focus our humiliations on such scapegoats—those who *must die* to ease our disgrace—we make them pay for our incapacity to deal with self-contempt and our unwillingness to address our terrible yet precious inadequacy. "We must project power. Inflate! Avoid!"

How the deuce can any of us pray when we're so fearful, irate, ashamed, and allergic to our exposed powerlessness? How can we see others clearly enough when we're terrified within? The good news (and not so good news) is that these dis-eases can become the very vehicles for Grace to set us on the *Path to Life*. In other words, we can learn to become "wounded healers." *We have to go through to get to.*

In the following pages I offer what I have discovered about that path. I propose a journey into the secret places, those recesses we assiduously avoid, to find ourselves located at the crossroads where Life and Death separate. Here, we sit with Bartimaeus the blind beggar. With him, we, too, rarely see what fuels our blindness. We don't notice what we avoid. We live half-lives without vision. And at the same time, infatuated with personal and corporate dramas, we know neither the Giver nor our true gifts. We overlook riches hidden in the secret places of our wounded creaturehood. So, we begin here at the crossroads. Blind and with divided hearts.

I propose that becoming aware of ourselves as blind in a world bathed in Light can become a joy. Discovering how we are pretenders to the throne may be liberating. Having our idolatries exposed could set us afresh on the *Path to Life*. God's grace can make use of every one of our flaws to draw us into the reconciling love of Christ. The most wonderful discovery in life involves seeing how we who claim to follow Christ are blind concerning everything and everyone, most especially God.

You may be wondering now: "Why would I want to read this? Start *where*?" Well, there are scores of books already published that focus on accepting our gifts, recognizing our blessings, and undergoing spiritual transformation. I simply wish to introduce the shadow side of our lives into the conversation. So, here it is. You be the judge. Notice what speaks to you. Leave the rest for further reads. Onward!

Know Thyself

Late have I loved you,
O Beauty ever ancient, ever new,
late have I loved you.
You were within me, and I was outside myself
and it was there that I sought you...
 ST. AUGUSTINE, CONFESSIONS 10

When St. Augustine became aware that he was living outside himself, he launched a more intense inward journey to find not only himself but also the God he thought he knew. He entered into his depths and ever more deeply into the divine mystery. Or rather, his search to connect deeply with God led him to embrace his own self-will and self-reliance, which he had yet to recognize.

"*You were within me, and I was outside myself and it was there that I sought you.*" Does he name your experience? He does mine. Long ago, Augustine identified our chronic predicament, the very dilemma that could launch our journeys to encounter God, self, and others anew.

It *is* probable our journeys will become narcissistically circumscribed quests for happiness or wholeness or security or self-esteem or even wisdom. Hold the presses! In fact, that's an excellent starting point! Perhaps, like Augustine, we begin outside ourselves, seeking *our selves* out there somewhere.

The arduous-yet-potentially-healing path from outside to inside naturally leads into the night, into our gloom, into the places where we are blind. It's like cautiously edging down the stairs into the basement, light dwindling, door closing behind, groping in our murky crypt. It seems a wintry place. Our frozen hearts reside there. There are things down there we haven't wanted to see, and for good reason. We have locked them away and lived our lives upstairs, outside, on the surface, in artificial light we can control.

Perhaps today is the day to notice the door that leads into those obscure depths. May courage and curiosity accompany you. Take with you a wise guide, a spiritual companion, a therapist who sees riches in your gloom. It is absolute folly to descend into night alone.

I intend the following study of Bartimaeus to gradually uncover some of what we have been blind to and, with divine grace over time, to bring them into the Light where some of the hurts, wounds, and sorrows can become the secret riches of our lives. Perhaps our frozen hearts will thaw a bit. If they melt, even a tad, we may be able to lift *our* burdens from the shoulders of our scapegoats.

A Modest Proposal

In the Exercises,
*"progress" in the spiritual life
is brought about in consolation*
(Spiritual Exercises, *316).*

◆¿ ADDRESS TO THE 36TH GENERAL CONGREGATION
OF THE SOCIETY OF JESUS BY POPE FRANCIS

On October 24, 2016, Pope Francis reminded the XXXVI General Congregation of the Society of Jesus, "Progress in the spiritual life is brought about in consolation." This saying is terribly counterintuitive to those of us who habitually need to prove our worth by trying harder. "I need to be more open in prayer. I shouldn't only ask for what I want. I must be more patient, pure, joyful, and generous. I must be a better _____ . I should be kinder. I ought not gossip about others. I shouldn't hold grudges. I need to *try harder, damn it.* You know this?

I believe most people who promote "trying harder" genuinely wish to encourage, motivate, inspire, challenge, and spark deeper spiritual living among the faithful. They say: "We/you should, we ought, we need to, we must, we had better…; if we only… then we would…." However, such intolerance of imperfection generates enough internal resistance to counteract and overthrow every good intention, every commitment to change. Anger at self for always being less than perfect never gives birth to the very transformation we seek. *Trying harder is self-defeating.*

I offer an idea to deal with this conundrum: we learn to inhabit our lives by surrendering our need to change. We leave transformation in God's hands by sitting with Bartimaeus at the crossroads. Here, two paths diverge. One leads toward deeper recognition of inner wounds and greater accountability for fears, resentments, and shame; the other to the path the scribes and Pharisees walked, on which we make others pay the price for our unseen hurts. Let's test whether God really *can* make everything work together for our good and the good of the world.

Immediately below I offer a brief illustration of what stepping onto the *Path toward Life* looks like. "There," I believe, is where we intend to go.

It's Where We Are Called—"There"
Here is my current favorite description of "there."

> Now on a day while he was riding over the plain that lieth beneath the city of Assisi, [Francis] met a certain leper, and this unforeseen meeting filled him with loathing. But when he recalled the purpose of perfection that he had even then conceived in mind, and remembered that it behooved

him first of all to conquer self, if he were fain to become the soldier of Christ, he leapt from his horse and ran to embrace him.

When the leper stretched forth his hand as though to receive an alms, he kissed it, and then put money therein. Then forthwith mounting his horse, he looked round him on all sides, and the plain was spread before him unbroken, and no trace of that leper might he see.

Then, filled with wonder and joy, he began devoutly to chant praises unto the Lord, purposing from this to rise ever unto greater heights.[1]

Francis leapt from his horse to embrace what he most feared: his inner leper, his poverty, his alienation. He met Christ there and was blessed with wonder and joy at this encounter. He praised the Lord for turning his commonsense world upside down and showing him how the *Way to Life* led through his aversion to poverty to the love of Christ *in* his poverty.

This portrait of Francis is at once an ideal and an antidote to idealism. We can take this ideal as an indictment of our lack of compliance: "You're not enough! Try harder! Then you'll be worthy. God will finally approve!" Or, by becoming aware of the distance we experience from the ideal, we could become willing to embrace ourselves *as we are*. Every burden can become its own antidote to shame as we progress in awareness of our patterns and God's mercy.

---

1 Saint Bonaventure, "Chapter One: Of His Manner of Life in the Secular State," *The Life of St. Francis of Assisi*, translated by E. Gurney Salter (New York: E.P. Dutton, 1904). Published on the internet by www.eCatholic2000.com: http://www.ecatholic2000.com/bonaventure/assisi/francis.shtml

Segue

Without God, we cannot.
Without us, God will not.
— ST. AUGUSTINE

Sighted people assume that all who cannot see as we do are blind. This is simply not the situation I address. Blindness serves here as a metaphor for the all-too-human unwillingness to recognize whatever wounds, hurts, and dis-eases keep us from recognizing God, ourselves, and others. We may someday discover that what we previously judged harshly in our lives and the lives of others are in truth hidden riches that can lead us to become "wounded healers." It's the journey inside-from-outside that's the kicker.

I still cling to the need to have God make my life absolutely joyful by taking care of all my problems. I have prayed for that since my youth. Didn't happen. Why doesn't God make me better? Why can't I make me better myself?

What I have come to see only recently is how sitting with Bartimaeus at the crossroads where Life and Death intersect discloses my situation: I get to choose which path to follow. And I get to explore whatever fuels my regular choice of the path toward Death—fears, resentments, etc. This is my starting point, our starting point as disciples. Grace continues to open the mystery of my all-too-human incompleteness, inadequacy, and shortcomings as I become willing to inhabit my life right here.

Let's take a seat here with Bartimaeus, the blind beggar. What does the *Path toward Death* look like? What does Jesus say about the *Way to Life*?

Chapter One

BLIND BY THE WAY

A Modest Proposal

The late Sebastian Moore, OSB, identified a subtle spiritual feint we humans use to domesticate God. It transforms religion into an effort to win God's favor and buttress our fragile self-esteem. We clutch at the illusion of perfecting ourselves to gain approval by the divine judge. We skew the Good News toward proving our worth: "at last the transcendent God has looked down and said, 'OK, you made it, I'm satisfied.'" This is the very picture of living on the outside.

> And it is exactly the reverse…It is the invasion of [humankind] by [Christ] with God at the center as love. But this total and final reversal takes place in the context

of the people we are, still conscious animals scared of our animality and seeking to ennoble ourselves.²

St. Francis kissed the leper to discover Christ. Like Francis, we could become aware of our "inner leper" and find a new willingness to meet Christ *in the midst of* our precious wounds. And to endure the pain of how we have wounded others as we become willing to make amends.

Adult spiritual practice quickens as we see we are blind to our self-will and charade. Mesmerized by distractions, habitual inattention, or unrelenting perfectionism, we avoid looking inward and do not realize how shame obscures the nature of our character defects, wrongdoings, sins, and unskillful behaviors *as well as* our true strengths and goodness.³

Bartimaeus the blind beggar will guide us. I have come to see him as *the* model of discipleship in the Gospel of Mark. He was poor. He couldn't see. He knew his situation. And, so, he begged to "look up" to see the *Way to Life*.

Onward and inward.

Our Foundational Image: Divine Comedy

I urge you to take this first image to heart. Post it on the lintels of your heart. In his masterpiece for the ages, the *Divine Comedy*, Dante Alighieri (d. 1321) journeys with the great poet Virgil among the broken and damned. Virgil guides him through the fires of purification to the sweetness of the beatific vision—a quest that begins *only* when Dante awakens to the realization that he had strayed and was lost:

---

2 Sebastian Moore, *The Crucified Jesus Is No Stranger* (Minneapolis, MN: The Seabury Press, 1977), pp. 48-49.

3 So many books deal with discovering our gifts; do seek one. I deal with discovering Christ in our woundedness.

*Middlemost through this life's journey, I wandered
from the straight path and awoke to find myself
lost and forsaken in a forest somber. How shall I tell*

*its true terror! I never saw so grim,
so noxious, so unyielding a wilderness!
Its harsh memory denotes fear itself.*

*Death—scarce more bitter a pill than that realm!
Amazing! good emerged from therein, I will tell
all God's grace did teach me there.*

*I remember not how I found my way,
restless, anxious, and discontent I had become
when I realized I had lost the One Path.*[4]

Dante had drifted and found himself at the gates of his personal hell. Virgil guides him into the depths of *inferno*, through *purgatorio*, and eventually to heaven's brink. He shows Dante the burdens of the hell-bound. He reveals to him the frozen defiance of Satan. He shows him the healing power of purification, the thawing of rebellion. He testifies how the melting of bitterness will free Dante to enter Glory. When Virgil delivers him to the gates of heaven, Dante's beloved Beatrice welcomes him.

Dante discovers how *everything* in his life has not only prepared him to enter the Presence, but how *everything*, purified and transformed, is, in fact, a beautiful gift to share. The insights of this great masterwork confirm what Dante had learned from St. Augustine—knowledge of God is intimately related to knowledge of self.

---

4 Dante Alighieri, "The Inferno: Canto I, verses 1-12" in *Divine Comedy*, my paraphrase.

We have all strayed. We may have even stood before the gates of hell and become appalled at our icy defiance. This is our starting point. Therefore, I urge you to hold onto Dante's journey as *the lens* through which to read this book. He embraced the journey of purification and walked toward the Light.

We'll do this together. It is folly to enter the gloomy valley without a wise guide and an ever-deepening experience of the mercy of God.

The following images bring to light aspects of blindness to which, I believe, you and I are, well… blind. The Light already surrounds us! My hope is that our exploration inward will prompt the journey upward.

First Image: The Dang Log

If you're anything like me, you resist the idea that you have trouble seeing clearly. And when Jesus challenges me, I don't always like it:

"Why do you see the speck in your neighbor's eye,
but do not notice the log in your own eye?
Or how can you say to your neighbor,
'Friend, let me take out the speck in your eye,'
when you yourself do not see the log in your own eye?"
LUKE 6:41–42; ALSO MATTHEW 7:3

Over the years, friends, fellow travelers, spiritual writers, and therapists have shined a light upon the many logs in my eye: burdened by shame, blind to my gifts and talents, discounting what drives me to act out, overlooking self-absorbed willful ways, disregarding how I earn and maintain my fragile self-esteem, rationalizing whatever impact I have on others—these are among them. I have minimized my real situation by living on the outside unwilling to look inside.

On so many levels I get it. So why do I habitually ignore Jesus' teaching? Because I live outside myself much of the time. I don't see. I operate as if what I see is objectively accurate and undeniably true, thank you very much. For example, I still blame a lot of folks for my wounds. I resent the harm they did to me. It's much easier to look at them than at myself.

Paradox: I am blind, yet act as if I see everything clearly. You?

I live every day blind to the redwood tree firmly planted in my eyes *because I don't notice it; I easily forget Jesus' words.* Spiritual Alzheimer's? Instead, I act like I can see the splinters in your eyes. (You should do something about them. Really. Let me help.) Thus, denial keeps me blind to myself. Nor do I see you for who you really are. I habitually overlook my part in things that have caused me pain.

Whom do I in fact see when I look at you? Yep. Me. And there's more. I beat you with that same log I use to club myself. You recognize it better. Ouch.

What follows is basically a report on the log in my eye, as best I can see it. It's right here in my eye as I sit beside Bartimaeus. (NB: When I say "I," I mean me. When I say "We," I'm generalizing from my experience.)

Second Image: The Dang Elephant

When my dad was in his final years, he developed macular degeneration. No more driving. He relied on my six sisters for day-to-day help. Once I visited him and he remarked on the differences between the six of them. "Ya know, I'll say something to one of them and get back five other versions. What was that story about different interpretations? Is it the one about the guys with macular degeneration who came upon an elephant? Was it this story? These six blind guys examined an elephant. Each stood around the great beast near the trunk, an ear, a leg, the tail, a tusk, or its belly. Each one tried to convince the other five that *his* reckoning absolutely defined the creature. But we know each dealt with only a portion of the mammal and mistook his segment for the whole." Yeah," my dad said, "it's like that."

Reality is what it is. How we interpret it is another thing altogether.

Why don't we get this?

Now, for the record, I am not a relativist. I'm simply applying Plato's paradox of the "One and the Many." Truth is absolute. It is one. Interpretations particularize the one truth. They are legion. For example, the United States is blessed with its constitution and amendments. Why so many opposing opinions? The Roman Catholic Church was influenced by Vatican II. How ought we account for so many incompatible interpretations—other than "everyone else is wrong"? Christians have one Bible. Why so many different understandings?

Blindness? Forgetfulness? Spiritual Alzheimer's? Me too.

Third Image: That Dang Inkblot

Let's add another principle: we interpret from out of our own personal vantage point and consider other possible ways of understanding reality second or third. Reality is *the* great inkblot test, eliciting profoundly personal and varied responses from each of us. We don't recognize how we interpret every person, every event from our inside out.

Though commonsense tells us otherwise, we don't reckon with the grids through which we judge *the meaning of* reality. And these exist within. Like the log in the eye, it is as highly personal as it is invisible. It "resides" in our minds and influences our attitudes and actions. The process of perceiving, understanding, and evaluating whatever is before us resembles interpreting an inkblot. And our starting point is "me."

Here is another wrinkle: the grid through which we engage reality is not only personal but also corporate. That is, the ideologically compatible group to which we each pledge allegiance shapes the framework through which we engage and interpret everything. Whether it's family, teachers, church, political party, or peers, we huddle with those who think like we do. We find security in sticking with like-minded folks. Our group grounds us. It insulates us. It endorses our right to scapegoat others who don't think like us.

Perhaps one day we may feel cramped by whichever confining vision we subscribe to. We may begin to wonder about the lens through which we interpret everything and evaluate reality. Realizing our blindness could position us to beg Christ to see.

Fourth Image: The Drama Zone
Outwardly focused, we miss how the log in our eye, our part of the elephant, and our highly patterned, chronic responses to reality point to unseen, inner processes that shape our dealings with what we call "the world." These all have become our habitual ways of organizing the chaos of reality.

Voilà! A fourth proposition: We followers of Jesus are actors on stages of our own making on which we play out inner dramas 24/7/365 based on time-worn scripts.

Happy scripts celebrate persons or events that gratify us. Angry scripts tether us to those we perpetually blame for our unhappiness. Fear-based scripts lead to fight, flee, or freeze. People or events provoke us. However, our recurrent-yet-unidentified scripts keep us outwardly focused on them *to avoid noticing and accounting for* whichever personal anxieties and resentments drive us. Here are several examples of "scripts" I deal with personally.

- "I act tough, angry, or cool to conceal my vulnerability."
- "I overwork to prove my worth, my value."
- "I buy things or overeat to feel full."
- "I maneuver others to alleviate my loneliness."
- "I bristle at others and blame them to avoid seeming weak."
- "I'm the best. God approves of me."
- "I'm ashamed. I bargain with God: 'At least I'm better than…/not as bad as I used to be.'"
- "I'm completely worthless. God rejects me."

Our scripts keep us focused outward. Self-esteem threatened? Blame someone. Self-will opposed? Batter them to comply. Vulnerability exposed? Inflate in anger to avoid feeling small. Insecurity, loneliness, a sense of inadequacy, fear of abandonment, or unworthiness provides raw material for our inner scriptwriters. Inner vulnerability, emptiness, fear of failing, and more all urge us toward center stage: "Let the show begin! Curtain! Up Music! Lights!" Suddenly, I'm special again—no longer beset by the pains and weaknesses of the moment. Dazzled by the lights, we take on a part we know well, reinforcing our inner blindness.

As we learn to read the text of our recurring scripts and learn to recognize what fuels our dramas, we can discover neglected parts of our lives to bring into the Light. As did Dante. The good news is that, at the word of God, Abram and Sarai left their land for a promised land. Moses led the people across the Red Sea. Saul, hunter of Christians, became St. Paul. What would it be like to go off-script to be directed by the divine scene-stealer?

INTERMISSION 1: A STORY! A STORY!

Hurt people hurt people.
— ANONYMOUS

I remember speaking with a dad after Mass about ten years ago or more. He was upset with himself and his teenage son. They had gotten into it before Mass. After he poured out his tale of regret and anger, I asked, "How much is your kid like you?" Everything changed. His shoulders slumped and his voice got softer. "He's a lot like me, and I don't want him to grow up to be like me or my old man." After listening more, I offered, "Thank God every day for that kid. He's pushing your buttons and uncovering your wounds. This may be your call to work on your own stuff so you don't lambaste him for reminding you of yourself."

Who ticks you off? Insert the name of the politician, religious leader, boss, coworker, spouse, relative, or child. None of them live to exasperate us (well, for the most part!). If or when this dad learns to read the text of his own life-script, he may discover something like: "I am ashamed that I didn't apply myself in school. I'm angry my dad didn't guide me. I feel inadequate. I resent my son for reminding me of me. I'm afraid he'll turn out like me."

That murky inner-world of fear, resentment, and unresolved grief led this good-yet-unseeing dad to castigate his son for his own stuff. The good news is that, should the dad begin to account for his own dramas, delve into them, and bring what fuels his scripts to the Light, he could see himself *and* his son more clearly. To put it another way: when we, like Augustine, are on the outside not looking inward, we punish others for our woundedness. "You displease me so much, I (feel entitled to) execute judgment. You are wrong and bad. I am in the right. I blame you. I punish you."

When we gain enough perspective to read the text of our own scripts and grasp what drives us, we may eventually grope for the Light.

Fifth Image: Guilt or Shame?
Guilt differs markedly from shame. Guilt acknowledges wrongs done; shame blinds with self-contempt. Always. Guilt says, "I did wrong." Or, "I was wrong when I…" Guilt recognizes the violation as relational. Shame implodes, "I'm bad." Or, "I'm unworthy…" We burrow into the cave of self-loathing with shame, our souls paralyzed. Guilt, however, can open us outward.

Guilt *could* lead to repentance, changing one's behavior or attitude, because the guilty person can see her situation more clearly without the paralyzing cloak of contempt. It is possible that when she becomes aware she's powerlessness to control her willful acting out, *her response to incompleteness*, she *may* become willing to bring her impotence to God and another she trusts. Not so with shame. With shame, the person becomes mired in the drama of self-flagellation-disguised-as-remorse. He takes refuge in the gloom, lurking in isolation from the Light.

Shame hijacks him on the way to the open door of mercy. His script, "Shame 24/7," kicks him into high gear, ever more absorbed with how undeserving of forgiveness he is. *I'm so stupid! I should have fixed myself yesterday! Try harder!* Blind to other options, his inner taskmaster requires he fix his life. Fix his life?

- Plumbers *fix* plumbing and car repairmen *fix* autos to make them work again.
- Lepidopterologists display butterflies by *fixing* them to boards with pins.
- Drug addicts look for a *fix* to avoid their pain.

- In the old-school manner of producing photographs from negatives, the chemical *fix* bath interrupts the development process.
- Pet owners *fix* their pets. Yep.

Conned by the illusion that trying harder will help him become acceptable, he remains blind to the vicious cycle he continually aggravates:

act out » shame » anxiety » tension » act out for relief » repeat

He doesn't see how looking at his patterns could lead him to the Light.

Being positive about our lives by noticing and affirming our strengths is essential. Suppressing our shame is folly. Rather, becoming aware of what fuels shame by tolerating the discomfort of emptiness, loneliness, abandonment, fear, inadequacy, unworthiness, and resentment opens a place for the Light of Christ. Perhaps one day, wearied by his dogged efforts, he may sit down beside Bartimaeus and beg to see.

Sixth Image: The Dang Hamster Wheel
The tyranny of perfectionism, often known as scruples, hobbles many of us. Perfectionists require themselves (and others!) to live in a state of irreproachable virtue…or else. Horrified by the mess in *their* lives, they beat the stuffing out of themselves (and others) to stave off condemnation from their harsh inner judge. What they put themselves through is unbearable. They respond by attempting to order their world to eliminate mistakes. Should they fail, these good people manage their anxiety by jumping on their inner hamster wheels and running with dire urgency. For many, this is *the unseen* pattern that has yet to be accounted for.

One script plays out in this theater—*Try harder! Justify yourself! You must be better. You* should *be better! Prove yourself worthy!* Perfectionists suffer this torment every day. A covert double bind surfaces, revealing the impossible burden they try to bear: Resenting *all* defects drives them to correct deficiencies *everywhere*. Yet failure to control their failings fuels impatience with self and others. Yet being impatient is wrong! On the wheel!

Running on that damnable wheel signifies "going nowhere faster." It embodies maximum effort coupled with the least possible amount of change. Why? Because, to alter anything implies imperfection. It's a frustrating standoff that effectively keeps a person blind to everything except the warped mirror that shows only blemishes, never beauty. Which in turn, sends repentance to the wings of the theater in favor of the script of self-justification driven by anxiety regulation. Was it Einstein who said, *Problems cannot be solved with the same mindset that created them?*

The good news is that God has made a remedy out of creatureliness itself.

Seventh Image: The Comfort Zone

I believe there is one [issue facing the new pope]
that is perhaps being overlooked,
but contains within it all these issues and
embodies the greatest threat to living the faith
and proclaiming Gospel values
to modern humanity:
the globalization of superficiality.
◐ CHRISTOPHER HALE, "THE GREATEST BATTLE FACING THE NEW POPE,"
AMERICA, MARCH 13, 2013[5]

---

5 http://www.americamagazine.org/content/all-things/greatest-battle-facing-next-pope

Here's what I demand: convenience, security, and to have the world mirror back to me whatever bolsters my self-esteem. You? Blind to our woundedness, we confirm our worth by seeing logs in others' eyes, our (illusion of) objectivity, the drama others create, (the illusion of) trying harder, and (the illusion of) self-justification. "Comfort zone" signifies that place of asylum we construct where we can feel well-defended, cozy, secure, and opaque. Safe in there, we believe we can ward off all that is annoying, threatening, and sinister.

Anxiously alert and outwardly focused in our fortresses, we relax behind the facade of safety. That is, our blindness affords us the simplistic charade of certainty in an uncertain world. The irony is that, because we remain wary of outside threats, we find little or no relief in our comfort zones. Numbed against our vulnerability, we distance ourselves from perilous intimacy with God, self, and others.

Our insecurity, the justification for our comfort zones, is not neutral. It fuels our decisions: to whom will I listen, whom ignore? With whom will I associate, whom spurn? Where will I shop, where avoid? What will I wear, whom belittle? With whom am I comfortable, whom exclude? Of whom am I jealous? The rich? Whom disdain? The poor? Living on the surface, we remain blind to who in fact needs care and attention.

INTERMISSION 2: A STORY! A STORY!

I have observed the following characteristics in the way some have dealt with the sacrament of reconciliation over the past thirty-seven years. Our protagonist said, "You can call me Al."

Al interpreted his life through a grid—like members of his broken (yet blessed) family do, and others who influenced him, including priests and nuns, peers—of Catholic "culture" and American "values." As he grew, Al worked their grids into his own. They told him sins are acts of omission and commission. He evaluated his life through the Ten Commandments, the laws of the church, and the seven Capital Sins (anger, sloth, pride, lust, envy, gluttony, and avarice). He confessed disobedience, fighting with brothers and sisters, laziness, lying, and talking back. He hit puberty. Then it was all about sex and anger.

Unseen shame cloaked Al's life. He always felt like he wasn't doing anything right. He ratcheted up his intentions higher and higher, especially when, each month or so, he felt impelled to go to confession. Without awareness of what fed his patterned behaviors, Al remained blind, living outside himself and amicably apart from God. He had not been taught to look deeper. Burdened by shame, he kept parts of his life hidden from others. He grew more aloof.

Somewhere in his forties, Al started noticing this or that patterned avoidance—imperfection, conflict, neediness, vulnerability, appearing unheroic, pain, and emptiness. He recognized them first in others. That's just the way it was. He evaded whichever segments of his life were too hot to handle, too painful to admit: loneliness, emptiness, insecurity, unworthiness, inadequacy, resentment, fear, and unresolved grief. Yet he had a hunch…

Al was unwilling to (and in fact could not) identify how he reacted to threats to his need to belong, his efforts to build self-esteem, his ambitions. He still had not perceived how his inner urgency to finagle emotional and material security drove him. His fundamental vulnerability was lost in the fog. Life, burdens, loss, and disappointment provided more than enough resentment toward God-who-didn't-save-him-from-suffering. It took a long, long time for Al to realize that he hadn't trusted God for a long time.

He began noticing what had been emerging in his life. He had dismissed them, "Ah, it's just a midlife crisis. I'll just get a

Porsche!" He struggled with restlessness, discontent, and irritability for more than a decade. He tried harder to get his life together. At some point, he realized he couldn't do it by himself. At another point, he became willing to seek outside himself for something other than sex, drugs, and rock 'n' roll.

He found trustworthy people to talk to. Al began bringing it all to the Light. He started to find freedom and some peace. It took a longer time to realize and admit he had harmed others as well. He had been so occupied by his own pain for decades that he just couldn't deal with the many he had hurt. He brought this new data to his confessor.

Al gradually discovered how powerless he was over not only his actions and attitudes, but the deeper wounds that drove him. These he also learned to bring to the Light—in prayer, in confession, and with a men's support group. Today Al is practically shocked to see how what he had previously repressed is becoming that which leads him to freedom to love others. Less encumbered by shame, he is more able and willing to address the things in his life that have driven him forever. He continues to redress as many wrongs as possible. He hands over his temptations, resentment, fears, will—everything—to God daily and often finds serenity and joy.

From Inferno to Purgatorio to Paradiso through…

Our study of the blind beggar situates us next to Bartimaeus at the crossroads. We will find friends here. Peter, James, John, Andrew walk nearby. They hardly recognize their resistance to Jesus' teaching and his mission yet somehow still seek the *Path to Life*. The scribes and Pharisees walk a separate path, firmly committed to the *Path toward Death*. Several whom Jesus healed are here too. And Bartimaeus sits beside the way today. He begged for sight when he heard Jesus approach. How might we respond here at our personal crossroads? What will we see, being blind and beggarly?

QUESTIONS TO BRING TO YOUR PRAYER

1. How do you react when someone or some event threatens your basic impulse to belong—companionship, self-esteem, status, acceptance, power, respect, prestige, fame, and recognition? What patterned responses arise? Does drama ensue? What fuels it?

2. How would you typically respond when persons or events jeopardize your emotional or material security? What scripts do you bring to the stage? Fear? Angry self-defense? Aggression? Resentment or vengeance? Uncertainty? Withdrawal? What lights the lights for more drama?

3. Shame encourages isolation, impeding our ability to call out for help. Have you grappled with shame in your life? Can you imagine crying out, like Bartimaeus, to ask for divine help to see your plight more clearly?

4. What do you think of the idea that learning to tolerate the discomfort of emptiness, loneliness, abandonment, fear, inadequacy, unworthiness, and resentment opens the place for the Light of Christ to shine?

5. What are your answers to these questions?
    - To whom am I willing to listen, whom ignore?
    - With whom will I associate, whom spurn?
    - Where will I shop, where avoid?
    - What will I wear to impress others, whom belittle because they don't pass judgment?
    - With whom am I comfortable, whom exclude?
    - Of whom am I jealous? The rich?
    - Whom disdain? The poor?

Chapter Two

WHICH WAY?

*"Pay no attention to that man behind the curtain...
Yes, I am a humbug."*
　🎵 **THE WIZARD IS FOUND OUT IN** *THE WIZARD OF OZ*

*We tend to be afraid of any knowledge
that could cause us to despise ourselves
or to make us feel inferior, weak,
worthless, evil, shameful.
We protect ourselves
and our ideal image of ourselves
by repression and similar defenses,
which are essentially techniques
by which we avoid becoming conscious*

*of unpleasant or dangerous truths.*⁶
ABRAHAM MASLOW, QUOTED IN *DENIAL OF DEATH*

Once I began having the speck of courage I needed to start looking at the log in my own eye (and didn't die!), I began to realize that as much as we reject our poverty and creatureliness, we remain blind *also* to Christ already dwelling in the mess, turmoil, and alienation in our hearts. We miss not only the possibility of saving encounters with Christ in our "stuff" but also the many ways God can use our temptations and failings to set us firmly on the *Path to Life*.

I have come to recognize Bartimaeus-as-disciple as an icon for discerning Christ's presence in our good and wounded lives. The passage about the blind beggar concludes Jesus' determined journey to Jerusalem. He had predicted his death, parried onslaughts from scribes and Pharisees, and feverishly taught his disciples the ways of the Reign of God.

All the while, the Gospel of Mark's stories have demonstrated the incapacity of Jesus' disciples to grasp the meaning of his mission. Thus, when Bartimaeus cried out for sight, he revealed himself as blind among the blind. And, when healed, he followed Jesus on the Way as the *first seeing disciple* in Mark. He will be our guide. Let's sit, then, with Bartimaeus beside the way and wonder, "Which *way* do I in fact walk?"

By the Way & On the Way

They came to Jericho.
As he and his disciples

---

6 Abraham Maslow, "The Need to Know and the Fear of Knowing," *Journal of General Psychology*, 1963, 68:119—as quoted in Becker, *Denial of Death*, pp. 51-52.

*and a large crowd were leaving Jericho,
Bartimaeus son of Timaeus,
a blind beggar,
was sitting by the roadside.*

🔊 SEE MARK 10:46–52

We first meet Bartimaeus sitting beside the *way*. Which way? It's ambiguous. He's simply sitting beside the way. He's at an intersection. "Two roads diverged…" and all that. Which way will he go? Which path will he choose? We have the privilege of sitting next to him during this study, blind beggars all. At the crossroads.

The Greek New Testament uses the word *hódos* (translated "way, path, route, road, roadside, or journey") to signify both the *Path to Life* and the *Path toward Death*. Mark sets Bartimaeus beside the *hódos*, the way. He is every disciple at the intersection where Life and Death contend.

Many translations interpret *hódos* as "the highway side" or "the road." But *hódos* has much deeper meaning, which we can uncover by looking at a few passages from the Septuagint (LXX), the Greek Old Testament that Mark had available to him.

Which Way?

The Septuagint contained a fixed number of words in its lexicon. I hold to the theory that each New Testament author culled specific terms from the wordlist of the sacred texts of Israel to express his unique way of understanding Jesus. That is, those writers we know as Paul, Matthew, Mark, Luke, John, James, Peter, and whoever wrote the Letter to the Hebrews interpreted the mystery of Jesus Christ from a distinct-yet-not-dissimilar perspective for their communities, drawing on the traditions of Judaism in which they were grounded.

Each author, therefore, promoted his own spiritual understanding of discipleship by choosing particular words to describe it. Let's put this thesis to the test by reviewing the potential meanings of *hódos* from which Mark could have drawn.

Hódos: A Significant Journey—From Slavery to Freedom

In the Pentateuch, the five books that make up the *Torah, hódos* often refers to a road that leads somewhere significant. It is first used when God drives out Adam and Eve: "and at the east of the garden of Eden he placed the cherubim and a sword flaming and turning to guard *the way* to the tree of life" (Genesis 3:24). It is used in passages about Noah, Abraham, Lot, Isaac, Jacob, Joseph and his brothers, Moses, and the nation Israel—and even God!—who each journeys along paths toward significant encounters.

In the Book of Exodus, *hódos* is used to describe Israel's journey from slavery to the false god Pharoah in Egypt to freedom and the true worship of God in the promised land. *Hódos* signifies a historical/theological/spiritual path. For example, at the shore of the Red Sea, the pillar of cloud led the people *along the way* out of Egypt to cross dryshod through the waters (Exodus 13:21). God promised, "I am going to send an angel in front of you *to guard you on the way* and to bring you to the place that I have prepared" (Exodus 23:20). Theirs was the spiritual journey of purification from idolatry (embodied in Pharoah-as-god and epitomized in their hankering for the "fleshpots of Egypt") toward belonging totally to God, their redeemer.

Exodus served as *the* foundation for Israel's covenant relationship: the faithful God led them along the *way* to true freedom. Second Isaiah put this image to use when he looked forward to a new Exodus as he encouraged the survivors of the Exile in Babylon to return to Jerusalem. He depicted a fresh journey from idolatry and oppression to freedom, from alienation to belonging.

> A voice cries out, "In the wilderness prepare *the way* of the LORD…Every valley shall be lifted up and every mountain and hill made low…" ISAIAH 40:3–4

> I am about to do a new thing; now it springs forth, do you not perceive it? I will make *a way* in the wilderness and rivers in the desert. ISAIAH 43:19

After the return of the exiles from Babylon, Nehemiah, the governor of the newly restored city, delegated Ezra the priest to read *Torah* to the people. By way of introduction to the reading, Ezra witnessed to God's saving power at the Red Sea *before*, as a sign of fidelity in their return from Exile *now*:

> Moreover, you led them by day with a pillar of cloud, and by night with a pillar of fire, to give them light *on the way* in which they should go. NEHEMIAH 9:12 (see v. 19 as well)

The Wisdom of Solomon (composed in the first century before Christ, it is also known as the Book of Wisdom in the Catholic lectionary) remembered Exodus to proclaim the providence of God in the face of Greek rulers' demands to worship other gods: Hold fast! Trust in God *now* who worked wonders for your ancestors *then*!

> The cloud was seen overshadowing the camp, and dry land emerging where water had stood before, *an unhindered way* out of the Red Sea, and a grassy plain out of the raging waves, where those protected by your hand passed through as one nation, after gazing on marvelous wonders.
> **WISDOM OF SOLOMON 19:7–8**

Hódos: The Way of God

The Book of Deuteronomy may have influenced later prophetic and wisdom literature in understanding *hódos* as *the way to walk rightly* before God. For example, it taught the practice of reciting *Shema* daily to help Israel remember that they still *walk the path* from slavery to freedom, and to warn them to shun worship of idols. Let us savor several morsels of this usage.

> You shall love the LORD your God with all your heart, and with all your soul, and with all your might. Keep these words that I am commanding you today in your heart. Recite them to your children and talk about them when you are at home and when you are *on the way*, when you lie down and when you rise.
>
> ◆ DEUTERONOMY 6:5–7; see also DT 11:19, 22F, 28; 30:16)

Lapsing represented forgetting; walking the *way* demonstrated remembering:

> So now, O Israel, what does the LORD your God require of you? Only to fear the LORD your God, *to walk in all his ways*, to love him, to serve the LORD your God with all your heart and with all your soul, and to keep the commandments of the LORD your God and his decrees that I am commanding you today, for your own well-being.
>
> ◆ DEUTERONOMY 10:12–13; SEE ALSO 11:19

The Wisdom literature encouraged the people to *walk in the way of God*, offering guidance for those on the *way*. Psalms, Proverbs, and Sirach are well known to most Christians. Ecclesiastes, Song of Songs, the Book of Job, and the Book of Wisdom may be less well known, yet offer detailed instruction, whether mundane advice…

> Go to the ant, you lazybones; consider its *ways* and be wise.
> ◆ PROVERBS 6:6

> Fools think *their own way* is right, but the wise listen to advice. ◆ PROVERBS 12:15

> Make no friends with those given to anger, and do not associate with hotheads, or *you may learn their ways* and entangle yourself in a snare. ◆ PROVERBS 22:24–25

or warnings against unrighteousness...

> The righteous gives good advice to friends, but *the way of the wicked* leads astray. *In the path of righteousness* there is life, *in walking its path* there is no death.
> ◆ PROVERBS 12:26, 28 (see also PSALM 25:8–10, 12)

or portraying an honorable life of wisdom...

> Whoever pursues [the *path* of] righteousness and kindness will find life and honor. ◆ PROVERBS 21:21

> Happy is the person who meditates on wisdom and reasons intelligently, who reflects in his heart on [Wisdom's] *ways* and ponders her secrets, pursuing her like a hunter, and lying in wait on her paths... ◆ SIRACH 14:20–22

Besides giving positive direction to Israel, wisdom literature also juxtaposed this path with the *Path (hódos) of Oppression and Idolatry.*

Hódos: The Path of Oppression & Idolatry

The final editor of the Book of Deuteronomy recognized the mystery of human woundedness and the many ways it distorts paths of fidelity into paths of faithless self-serving. As the book concludes, Moses foretells how this stiff-necked people would stray again from the way and predicts dire consequences.

> [Moses said:] "Assemble to me all the elders of your tribes and your officials, so that I may recite these words in their hearing and call heaven and earth to witness against them. For I know that after my death you will surely act corruptly, turning aside *from the way* that I have commanded you. In time to come trouble will befall you, because you will do what is evil in the sight of the Lord..."
> DEUTERONOMY 31:28–29

Biblical authors had long discerned the all-too-human tendency to stray from the *way*—Adam and Eve, Cain and Abel, Noah and the rest of the world, Abram and Sarai, Isaac, Jacob, and the brothers of Joseph. Even before there was an explicit *way* to follow (the commands given to Moses), time and again, humans strained the bonds of relationship with God and neighbor. Self-will expressed itself in self-worship (idolatry) and domination of others.

> Now the earth was corrupt in God's sight, and the earth was filled with violence. And God saw that the earth was corrupt; for *all flesh had corrupted its ways* upon the earth. And God said to Noah, "I have determined to make an end of all flesh, for the earth is filled with violence because of them..." GENESIS 6:11–13

The stories in the books of Exodus and Deuteronomy witness to Israel's susceptibility to stray from the path. For example, while Moses absented himself on the mountain forty days with the Lord, the people below reverted to old *ways*, fabricating a golden calf to worship (abandonment fears?). When he discovered this, Moses seethed. He broke the stone tablets and cried, "Then I saw that you had indeed sinned against the LORD your God, by casting for yourselves an image of a calf; you had been *quick to turn from the way* that the LORD had commanded you" (Deuteronomy 9:16 and Exodus 32:1ff).

Just so, from Moses to Samuel and Nathan, from Elijah and Elisha to Hosea, Amos, Isaiah, Jeremiah, and Ezekiel, prophets called the people of God back from idolatry…

> I have sent to you all my servants the prophets, sending them persistently, saying, "*Turn now everyone of you from your evil way*, and amend your doings, and do not go after other gods to serve them, and then you shall live in the land that I gave to you and your ancestors." But you did not incline your ear or obey me.   ◦᷅ JEREMIAH 35:15

> Later generations have seen the light of day, and have lived upon the earth; but they have not learned the way to knowledge, *nor understood her paths*, nor laid hold of her. Their descendants *have strayed far from her way*.
> ◦᷅ BARUCH 3:20–21

and from oppression of the poor to the way of righteousness and justice. Consider: What wounds could fuel thoughts of iniquity, desolation, and destruction, lack of peace within and refusal of justice without as triggers for violence? What needed healing?

> Thus says the LORD: For three transgressions of Israel, and for four, I will not revoke the punishment; because they sell the righteous for silver, and the needy for a pair of sandals—they who trample the head of the poor into the dust of the earth, and push the afflicted *out of the way*...
> ◆៛ AMOS 2:6–7

> Their feet run to evil, and they rush to shed innocent blood; their thoughts are thoughts of iniquity, desolation and destruction are in their highways. *The way of peace* they do not know, and there is no justice *in their paths*. *Their roads* they have made crooked; no one who walks in them knows peace. ◆៛ ISAIAH 59:7–8

Generation to generation, the Lord cajoled, summoned, and threatened the nation to get its attention to turn away from oppression and idolatry and *walk in the way* to which they had committed when they first received the commandments.

> Today you have obtained the LORD's agreement: to be your God; and for you to *walk in his ways*, to keep his statutes, his commandments, and his ordinances, and to obey him.
> ◆៛ DEUTERONOMY 26:17

The Hebrew Scriptures offer much more than a compilation of laws. They provide historical narrative, pithy sayings, a broad range of prayers, and commands that called the people—and now call us—to walk prudently in the *way* of the Lord.

Hódos: The Path of Wisdom
The Septuagint used *hódos* to illustrate the *path* of Wisdom. Here are four features I think worthy of note. Which of these

themes might apply to the Gospel of Mark and the story of Bartimaeus?

1. Those who delight in the Law of the Lord (Wisdom) and follow her ways are happy, for the Lord watches over the just. Daily meditation on the Word directs their path.

> Happy are those who do not follow the advice of the wicked, or *take the path* that sinners tread, or sit in the seat of scoffers; but their delight is in the law of the Lord, and on his law they meditate day and night. ❧ PSALM 1:1–2
>
> For the Lord watches over *the way of the righteous*, but *the way of the wicked* will perish. ❧ PSALM 1:6
>
> I said, "*I will guard my ways* that I may not sin with my tongue; I will keep a muzzle on my mouth as long as the wicked are in my presence."
> ❧ PSALM 39:1 (see PSALM 44:18)

2. Wisdom herself is a worthy guide. She shines forth; wickedness is gloom.

> She gave to holy people the reward of their labors; *she guided them along a marvelous way*, and became a shelter to them by day, and a starry flame through the night.
> ❧ WISDOM OF SOLOMON 10:17
>
> Why do you spend your money for that which is not bread, and your labor for that which does not satisfy?

> Listen carefully to me, and eat what is good, and delight yourselves in rich food. Incline your ear, and come to me; listen [*to my way*], so that you may live. ISAIAH 55:2–3

> Let the wicked *forsake their way*, and the unrighteous their thoughts; let them return to the LORD, that he may have mercy on them, and to our God, for he will abundantly pardon. For my thoughts are not your thoughts, *nor are your ways my ways*, says the LORD. For as the heavens are higher than the earth, *so are my ways* higher *than your ways* and my thoughts than your thoughts.
> ISAIAH 55:7–9 (see also PROVERBS 4:18)

3. You show me the way. Lead me and teach me, O LORD. Wait for the LORD.

> Let me hear of your steadfast love in the morning, for in you I put my trust. *Teach me the way* I should go, for to you I lift up my soul. PSALM 143:8 (see PSALMS 5:8; 27:11)

> You show me *the path of life*. In your presence there is fullness of joy; in your right hand are pleasures forevermore. PSALM 16:11

> I will instruct you *and teach you the way* you should go; I will counsel you with my eye upon you. Do not be like a horse or a mule, without understanding, whose temper must be curbed with bit and bridle, else it will not stay near you. PSALM 32:8–9

> Thus says the Lord, your Redeemer, the Holy One of Israel:
> I am the Lord your God, who teaches you for your own
> good, *who leads you in the way* you should go.
> ▪ ISAIAH 48:17 (see also PROVERBS 4:10; 6:23;
> PSALM 25:8–12; ISAIAH 35:8; 40:3; 42:16F)

4. Restore me, O God, from walking blindly the road to destruction.

> Their feet run to evil, and they rush to shed innocent
> blood; their thoughts are thoughts of iniquity, desolation
> and *destruction are in their highways. The way of peace* they
> do not know, and there is *no justice in their paths. Their roads
> they have made crooked*; no one who walks in them knows
> peace. ▪ ISAIAH 59:7–8

> Why have they been numbered among the children of
> God? And why is their lot among the saints? So it was
> *we who strayed from the way of truth*, and the light of
> righteousness did not shine on us, and the sun did not rise
> upon us. We took our fill of the *paths of lawlessness and
> destruction*, and we *journeyed* through trackless deserts, *but
> the way of the* Lord we have not known.
> ▪ WISDOM OF SOLOMON 5:5–7

> Restore to me the joy of your salvation, and sustain in me
> a willing spirit. *Then I will teach transgressors your ways*, and
> sinners will return to you.
> ▪ PSALM 51:12–13

Summary & Segue

Four hundred and thirty years after Joseph was sold into slavery in Egypt, Moses led Israel out of slavery to freedom. God made a covenant with this people, the very ones who had been formed into idolaters during their sojourn in Egypt. Ever since, we who walk in the Judeo-Christian way struggle with letting go of our idols. To this day, the invitation to walk the *hódos* of God calls to us. We struggle to respond. On the one hand, we, like the servants of old, ask "O Lord, teach me your paths." On the other, we continue to be unteachable, prone to violence, and fettered to our blindness with passionate resistance.

So, we find ourselves alongside Bartimaeus sitting at the crossroads. One path leads to worshiping God; the other to worshiping idols. One leads toward loving God and neighbor; the other to oppressing the poor. Which do we habitually choose? Exile or belonging? Self-giving or self-serving? Can we even see?

We cannot look far down either path; each is shrouded in fog. The *Path toward Death* is hidden by denial. The *Path to Life* is blanketed by blind resistance. Perhaps the very crossroads we're sitting at is obscured. What if we can't even see ourselves? Great! What an excellent starting point! We are still blind beggars beside the *way*, remember. And the divine physician approaches.

Let's continue our study: How did the Marcan Jesus apply the ideals laid out in the Jewish Scriptures, using the Septuagint's *hódos*? What was new? What similar? Next, we explore how Jesus illuminates the path for us in a profound and life-changing way.

QUESTIONS TO BRING TO YOUR PRAYER

1. Looking at the word *hódos* as used by the ancient Israelites reminds us that much of that with which we struggle has long been part of the human condition.
   - When you think of the struggle to move from slavery to freedom in our age, what comes to mind?
   - Are there any places in life in which you feel enslaved?
   - What would emancipation look like? Might it resemble Jesus' vision for human freedom?

2. We are invited to listen to the prophets and to discern the way of life.
   - Where do you hear prophetic voices today?
   - Do the sacred texts handed down to us across the generations speak to you? If so, how?
   - How clearly do you see yourself at this juncture of your life?

3. What is your reaction to the idea that there is a path of Truth and many, many interpretations of it? What principles do we use to discern how closely our hallowed views approximate Truth?

4. What is your reaction to the idea that we are sitting at the crossroads with one path leading to worshiping God and the other to worshiping idols? One that leads toward loving God and neighbor; the other to oppressing the poor? How will we know which path we walk?

Chapter Three

BLIND BEGGAR BY THE WAY

Who is this blind beggar who sits beside the way? We're not told a lot, are we?

Bartimaeus son of Timaeus, a blind beggar, was sitting by the way...He sits there not seeing. He's not anticipating a saving encounter with Jesus, just begging. Let's sit with him at the crossroads beside the *way*.

In this chapter, I'm going to continue to take a close, almost academic, look at the Greek words that Mark uses when he describes Bartimaeus. At times, it may almost feel like you're in a Scripture class! But I have found that digging out the original meaning of these words and looking at how they are used elsewhere in the Scriptures is incredibly illuminating. So hang in there with me as we take a dive into networks of meanings and connotations Mark establishes through his choice of

Greek terms. I hope to uncover new understandings of spiritual blindness.

Who is Blind? A First Look

The word used in the Greek version of the Scriptures for "blind" is *tuphlós*. Torah commanded care for the blind: "you shall not… put a stumbling block before *the blind*; you shall fear your God" (Leviticus 19:14). It is also used to describe a category of defects that excluded some from offering ritual sacrifice to God. (See Leviticus 21:18ff; Deuteronomy 15:21.) The word is mainly used, however, to describe the dangers of spiritual blindness. For example, toward the end of the book of Deuteronomy, Moses warns Israel of such perils. Turning to idols, they will experience abandonment. Lost, they will wander in a state of constant vulnerability. (See Deuteronomy 28:15, 28–29.)

Isaiah, continuing the Mosaic prophetic tradition, further specifies the meaning of spiritual blindness for the people: idolatry, oppression, and willfulness.

> Therefore, justice is far from us, and righteousness does not reach us; we wait for light, *and lo! there is darkness; and for brightness, but we walk in gloom. We grope like the blind* along a wall, *groping like those who have no eyes*; we stumble at noon as in the twilight, among the vigorous as though we were dead…for our transgressions before you are many, and our sins testify against us. ISAIAH 59:9–12

Still, it's not all dire. Isaiah also announces God's promise to open Israel's eyes. The prophet foretells an end to the exile and alienation that have resulted from idolatry. The people are promised salvation, light, life, healing of grief, end of fear, and the beginning of joy—and "*the eyes of the blind shall be opened*!" (Isaiah 35:5).

Idolatry and Spiritual Blindness: Wisdom 15—17

Catholics and Orthodox include the Wisdom of Solomon (also called the Book of Wisdom) in their Bibles. Written in Greek during either the second or first century BCE, the author of Wisdom understood the world as hostile to Jews, enticing them toward Greek culture and the worship of idols. In light of this concern, passages in this book brilliantly connect spiritual blindness and idolatry.

In chapter fifteen, the writer (some say it was King Solomon) exposed the futility of makers of idols in silver, gold, copper, or clay. Chapter seventeen applies the lens of Israel's bondage in Egypt thirteen hundred years earlier to indict first-century BCE Greek oppression: worshiping false gods meant living in perpetual blindness and terror at *everything*. The chapter concludes with a remarkable insight contrasting fear-idolatry-oppression-blindness with fidelity-sight.

> For the whole world was illumined with brilliant light, and went about its work unhindered, while over those people alone heavy night was spread, an image of the darkness that was destined to receive them; *but still heavier than darkness were they to themselves*. WISDOM 17:20–21

Paranoia reigned in the hearts of idolaters who would not recognize the chains that bound them—inward weakness, forgetfulness, cowardice, distress, drama, and burden of self. Then as now, all creation is bathed in bright light while terror weighs down all idolaters. Then as now, people could be spiritually blind and not even recognize it.

Segue to the Blind Beggar

Now, no one I know regards Bartimaeus as an idolater; he just couldn't see. Nonetheless, the Septuagint equates *spiritual* blindness with idolatry and oppression over and over again. What if Bartimaeus is not just sightless but is also blind in this biblical sense and cries out for vision? I think this twofold meaning makes sense because, upon gaining sight, he follows Jesus along the way, the *Path to Life*.

Let's take a moment to look from that dual vantage point: blind and idolatrous. With that second reality added in, how comfortable is it to sit next to Bartimaeus? I'm right there with you. Uncomfortable. Our study continues.

Bartimaeus—Sitting By the Way

Remember that *hodós* means "the way," the road or roadside, a trip or journey. Since we have already reviewed its use in the Septuagint, let's consider the gospel writer's characterization of *the way* by which Bartimaeus sat.

The word *hodós* appears in multiple passages in Mark, and given that this gospel emerges from an entirely Jewish corner of early Christianity, it's not surprising that we hear echoes of the Septuagint in its uses. For example, John the Baptist prepares the *Way to Life*, echoing the ancient summons of Isaiah. "Turn away from idolatry, oppression, and blindness!"

> As it is written in the prophet Isaiah, "See, I am sending my messenger ahead of you, *who will prepare your way*; the voice of one crying out in the wilderness: '*Prepare the way of the Lord*, make his paths straight.'" ◂ MARK 1:2–3

"Every valley shall be lifted up and every mountain and hill be made low" (Isaiah 40:4) completes the above quotation. Mark's choice of words links raising *valleys* with the savagery of idolatry condemned by the prophets in LXX:

> They built the *high places of Baal in the valley of the son of Hinnom,* to offer up their sons and daughters to Molech, though I did not command them, nor did it enter my mind that they should do this abomination, causing Judah to sin.
> 🔖 JEREMIAH 32:35

Throughout the gospel, Jesus regularly elicits resistance from his disciples as they travel *on the way.* It's counterintuitive. The way is the place of the unveiling of resistance. Yikes!

> Jesus went on with his disciples to the villages of Caesarea Philippi; *and on the way he asked his disciples…*"But who do you say that I am?" Peter answered him, "You are the Messiah…" And Peter took him aside and began to rebuke him. But turning and looking at his disciples, he rebuked Peter and said, "Get behind me, Satan! For you are setting your mind not on divine things but on human things."
> 🔖 MARK 8:27–33

> Then they came to Capernaum; and when he was in the house he asked them, *"What were you arguing about on the way?"* But they were silent, *for on the way they had argued with one another* who was the greatest. 🔖 9:33–34

> *As he was setting out [on the way],* a man ran up and knelt before him, and asked him, "Good Teacher, what must I do to inherit eternal life?"…Jesus, looking at him, loved him and said, "You lack one thing; go sell what you own, give the money to the poor, and you will have treasure

> in heaven"...Then Jesus looked around and said to his disciples, "How hard it will be for those who have wealth to enter the kingdom of God!" And the disciples were perplexed at these words... 🔊 10:17–24

> *They were [on the way]*, going up to Jerusalem, and Jesus was walking ahead of them; they were amazed, and those who followed were afraid. He took the twelve aside again and began to tell them what was to happen to him, saying, "See, we are going up to Jerusalem, and the Son of Man will be handed over..." 🔊 10:32–33

At every step of *the way*, the disciples demonstrate absolutely imperfect adherence to Jesus' mission and total non-compliance with his teaching. No paragons of virtue here! Nada. Zip. Yet, they keep following Jesus. They continue to listen to him. What a mystery! Could it be that they felt truly seen as they were *and* called forth into his light? I'd say yes, because I believe that's what happens on *the way*!

In the Gospel of Mark, Jesus' teaching about the way refers both to the *Way to Life* he proclaims and *the very path* on which he encounters real people, who are burdened, resistant, and blind. Mark's iteration of the parable of the sower illuminates this. It paints a realistic picture of the challenges of the word to bear fruit even among those who are on *the way*, the path of discipleship:

> The sower sows the word. *These are the ones on the path* where the word is sown: when they hear, Satan immediately comes and takes away the word that is sown in them. And these are the ones sown on rocky ground: when they hear the word, they immediately receive it with

joy. But they have no root, and endure only for a while; then, when trouble or persecution arises on account of the word, immediately they fall away. And others are those sown among the thorns: these are the ones who hear the word, but the cares of the world, and the lure of wealth, and the desire for other things come in and choke the word, and it yields nothing. And these are the ones sown on the good soil: they hear the word and accept it and bear fruit, thirty and sixty and a hundredfold. 4:14–20

Lucky for us, Jesus works with us as we are. And when we can see who we are, we discover the tensions of adult discipleship—seeing yet still idolatrous, unfruitful and yet fruitful. Following Christ *as we are* is the key. It entails surrendering our petrifying burden of unworthiness so we might hear, "You are my Beloved. Repent!"

Bartimaeus Cried Out beside the Way

Mark describes the wail of Bartimaeus with the word *krádzo*, "to shout, howl, cry out." In choosing this word, Mark identifies Bartimaeus with others in the gospel who also cry out. Throughout the gospel narrative, Jesus' appearance calls forth from those crowded around him the powerful resistance, brokenness, and pained longing that needs his healing.

> For he had cured many, so that all who had diseases pressed upon him to touch him. Whenever the unclean spirits saw him, *they fell down before him and shouted*, "You are the Son of God!" 3:10–11

Night and day among the tombs and on the mountains *he was always howling* and bruising himself with stones. When he saw Jesus from a distance, he ran and bowed down before him; *and he shouted at the top of his voice*, "What have you to do with me, Jesus, Son of the Most High God? I adjure you by God, do not torment me." 5:5–7

Immediately the father of the child cried out, "I believe; help my unbelief!" When Jesus saw that a crowd came running together, he rebuked the unclean spirit, saying to it, "You spirit that keeps this boy from speaking and hearing, I command you, come out of him, and never enter him again!" *After crying out and convulsing him terribly*, it came out... 9:24–26

They shouted back, "Crucify him!" Pilate asked them, "Why, what evil has he done?" *But they shouted all the more*, "Crucify him!" 15:13–14

Bartimaeus' cry stands in continuity with these other cries. We can think of him as crying out not only in belief but also on behalf of those who are in pain (*Help my unbelief!*) and those who worship idols (*Away with him!*).

Bartimaeus Was Looking Up on the Way

In our English translations of the story, Jesus calls Bartimaeus over and asks what he wants. Bartimaeus replies, "That I may see again!" But the Greek word used for the seeing he longs for is *anablépo*, which means "to look up or look back." It is curious that this is the *only* passage in the entire NRSV that translates the word *anablépo* as "to see again." Why, we might ask, does the gospel writer use *anablépo* here rather than the many other possible words that can be translated "to see" (and there are a lot of them: *blépo, blémma, diablépo, eidon, emblépo, epiblépo, theoréo, horáo*, etc.)?

Let's start, once again, with the Jewish roots of the gospel. The Septuagint tends to use *anablépo* at significant moments that reveal divine covenant fidelity:

> The LORD said to Abram, after Lot had separated from him, *"Raise your eyes now, and look from the place where you are…* for all the land that you see I will give to you and to your offspring forever." GENESIS 13:14–15

> But the word of the LORD came to him [and]…brought him outside and said, *"Look toward heaven and count the stars,* if you are able to count them." Then he said to him, "So shall your descendants be." GENESIS 15:4–5

> *On the third day Abraham looked up and saw the place far away.* Then Abraham said to his young men, "Stay here with the donkey; [Isaac] and I will go over there…[God] said, "Do not lay your hand on the boy or do anything to him; for now I know that you fear God, since you have not withheld your son, your only son, from me." *And Abraham looked up and saw a ram*…and took the ram and offered it up as a burnt offering instead of his son.
> GENESIS 22:4–13

What would this passage describing the request of Bartimaeus mean if the word was translated consistently with these other uses? What if *a return to covenant fidelity* is what Bartimaeus seeks, biblically speaking? Consider the other places that *anablépo* appears in this gospel:

> *Taking the five loaves and the two fish, he looked up to heaven,* and blessed and broke the loaves, and gave them to his

disciples to set before the people; and he divided the two fish among them all. 🕮 6:41

He took him aside in private, away from the crowd, and put his fingers into his ears, and he spat and touched his tongue. *Then looking up to heaven*, he sighed and said to him, "Ephphatha," that is, "Be opened." 🕮 7:33–34

They had been saying to one another, "Who will roll away the stone for us from the entrance to the tomb?" *When they looked up*, they saw that the stone, which was very large, had already been rolled back. As they entered the tomb, they saw a young man, dressed in a white robe… 🕮 16:3–5

Could it be that Bartimaeus is asking not merely for sight, but to see how he is immersed in the all-embracing covenant fidelity of God revealed in Jesus? Hmmm.

Bartimaeus Was Saved on the Way

"Go your way, your faith has made you well [saved you]!" The verb used here, *sózo*, means both "to heal" and "to save." Does Mark mean that the faith of the blind beggar saved him or healed him? Yes!

It makes sense to translate *sózo* as "to heal" when Jesus dealt with the man with a withered hand (3:3f), Jairus' daughter (5:23f), and the woman with the hemorrhage (5:28, 34f). Each of these events occurred *before* Peter declared, "You are the Messiah" (8:27–38). Because there are two Greek verbs translated "to heal," it's important to pay attention. Only one can be translated, "to save." The *Way to Life* certainly involves healing. It also means engaging Jesus' saving word—handing over one's life for the gospel, forsaking the lure of riches, enduring betrayal and rejection.

> *For those who want to save their life will lose it*, and those who lose their life for my sake, and for the sake of the gospel, *will save it.* ◁⟩ 8:35

> "It is easier for a camel to go through the eye of a needle than for someone who is rich to enter the kingdom of God." They were greatly astounded and said to one another, "*Then who can be saved?*" Jesus looked at them and said, "For mortals it is impossible, but not for God; for God all things are possible." ◁⟩ 10:25–27

> Brother will betray brother to death, and a father his child, and children will rise against parents and have them put to death; and you will be hated by all because of my name. *But the one who endures to the end will be saved.*
> ◁⟩ 13:12–13

Bartimaeus is saved/healed by Jesus and follows him, having lifted his eyes to recognize the covenant fidelity of God. He hands over his life for Jesus' sake and the sake of the gospel.

Seeing means following Jesus' way; it signifies salvation, which involves losing one's life, surrendering one's possessiveness, letting go one's demand to rule, and walking with Jesus to the cross…and receiving the healing of his resurrection.

As his followers, we believe that baptism establishes and grounds the disciple's commitment to the *way*:

> And he said to them, "Go into all the world and proclaim the good news to the whole creation. The one who believes and is baptized *will be saved*; but the one who does not believe will be condemned." ◁⟩ 16:15–16

So, here I am, sitting beside Bartimaeus where the roads fork off, one way toward Life and one way toward Death. I don't want to believe I have come to this crossroads from the *Path toward Death*. And I don't much like the *way* Jesus calls me to follow. Too much to let go of. Still, I want to go with him.

As I listen, Jesus seems altogether too much. He threatens my security, my ambitions, my self-will, my drive toward prestige. I keep my mind dull and my heart protected from his heart-breaking teaching. I'd rather maintain my "stuff," my riches and reputation. I'd rather not lose my life to save it, thank you very much. *Who can be saved?* Isn't there a way to follow him and *not see* how like Bartimaeus I am, blind and beggarly? I'd go for that. Yet he knows me and speaks to my soul.

So, we sit here with Bartimaeus and the Twelve and the other disciples, our new best friends forever, at the juncture.

QUESTIONS TO BRING TO YOUR PRAYER

1. There is a path toward life and one toward death. Which do you walk in your journey? Which path have you been traveling?
   - Do you walk the talk? Or, would like to better someday?
   - Are you still walking, or have you plopped down on the ground like Bartimaeus?

2. What comes to mind when you think about the need to cry out to God, like Bartimaeus did?
   - Do you feel resistant to showing that kind of vulnerability, even weakness?
   - Do you usually call to others and to God?
   - What would it be like to "shout, howl, or cry out"?
   - If you did, what would you cry out about?

3. In many situations in life, we find ourselves looking down, not up. We don't want to engage and make eye contact. Or we don't want to have to see things that will distress, disrupt, or disturb us.
   - If you were to use Bartimaeus' prayer to God, that you might "anablépo," what areas of your life would you want healed?
   - What would you want to see? What would you not want to see?
   - How might sight bring deeper fidelity to your life?

4. Mark's gospel uses the same word for healing and for saving. In our age, where many resist the idea that we are sinful and need to be saved, it may feel easier to pray for healing.
   - How do you relate to these words?
   - Do you have it in you to cry out for God to save you?
   - From what?

Chapter Four

BLIND DISCIPLES— WHICH WAY?

*But the path of the righteous
is like the light of dawn,
which shines brighter until full day.
The way of the wicked
is like deep darkness;
they do not know
what they stumble over.*
◆᷅ PROVERBS 4:18–19

Chapter 6. Against False Teachers…
For if you are able

*to bear the entire yoke of the Lord,
you will be perfect;
but if you are not able to do this,
do what you are able.*[7]

◂◉ DIDACHE 6:1–2

"Choose your Path!"

Scripture addressed people with divided hearts then as it continues to speak to us *today*: Worship the one God. Forsake injustice. Love your neighbor. This is the *Path to Life*. Turn away from the *Path toward Death*; forsake idolatry and oppression of the poor. Deuteronomy summed up this call to biblical wisdom: "I have set before you life and death…Choose life!" (30:19).

Jesus appears on the scene as the divine Rorschach, evoking forceful reactions from *everyone*—unclean spirits, the sick, sinners, scribes, Pharisees, disciples, and the Twelve. Their reactions reveal which path they habitually walk. Only those who become aware of their woundedness and need for healing become willing to bring themselves into the Light and beg to see. As does our exemplar Bartimaeus.

How does Mark apply the ancient summons to choose life and reject death? Does his gospel bring anything new to this enterprise? Let's take a look by looking yet again at the deep meaning of a word he uses to describe how people react to Jesus: *thélo*.

The Two Paths in the Second Gospel

A study of how Mark uses the Greek verb *thélo* ("to wish, want, choose, desire, be willing") gives us insight into people's attraction and aversion to Jesus, his person and mission. Each response

---

[7] *The Didache, the Teaching of the Twelve Apostles, 6:1–2*. Alexander Roberts, DD & James Donaldson, LL.D translation http://www.earlychristianwritings.com/text/didache-hoole.html

Jesus elicits from those with whom he is engaging reveals the person's fundamental orientation toward one or the other of the *Two Paths*. This is true for the disciples, the Twelve, the scribes, and the Pharisees. And, I suggest, ultimately each of us. Let's take a look, first, at the way the Jewish Scriptures speak of wishing, wanting, desiring, and more.

Thélo in the Septuagint

Israel intended to live as a grateful heir of their generous God and the gracious steward of a bounteous land. They resolved to live justly. They committed themselves to be thankful, forsake all idols, and offer praise only to their Redeemer. Nevertheless, while Israel sought divine favor, it too often practiced benign neglect. What happened to all these noble intentions?

Consider the following dialogue I've constructed based on the more than five hundred instances of *thélo* in the Septuagint. I've selected a number of them, and shaped them in a way that I think sheds light on Israel's elemental desires and the fundamental relationship between God and the chosen people.

God addressed the nation,
"Come, O children, listen to me; I will teach you the fear of the LORD. *Which of you desires life?* (Psalm 34:11–12). I will show you the way of living you seek, the way that will bring you interior peace and outward harmony. Trust me. Listen and live!"

And the people answered,
"For you are not a God *who delights* in wickedness..." (Psalm 5:4). We believe what the prophet Ezekiel told us, "I take no pleasure in [*do not desire*] the death of the wicked..." (Ezekiel 18:23–24). You told us openly to "get [yourselves] a new heart and a new spirit! Why will you die, O house of Israel? *For I have no pleasure*

in the death of anyone, says the Lord God. Turn, then, and live" (Ezekiel 18:31–32). You said you *"desire* steadfast love and not sacrifice, the knowledge of God rather than burnt offerings" (Hosea 6:6). *"You have no delight* in sacrifice…The sacrifice acceptable to God is a broken spirit; a broken and contrite heart, O God, you will not despise" (Psalm 51:16–17).

Create in us that new heart for "there is nothing on earth that *I desire* other than you. My flesh and my heart may fail, but [you are] the strength of my heart and my portion forever" (Psalm 73:25–26). Therefore, "lead me in the path of your commandments, for *I delight in* [your law]. Turn my heart to your decrees, and not to selfish gain" (Psalm 119:35–36).

Your Wisdom always seeks our good: "Although you are sovereign in strength, you judge with mildness, and with great forbearance you govern us; for you have the power to act whenever *you choose*. Through such works you have taught your people that the righteous must be kind, and you have filled your children with good hope, because you give repentance for sins"(Wisdom of Solomon 12:18–19).

And you told us we have freedom to choose the good: "If *you choose*, you can keep the commandments, and to act faithfully is a matter of your own choice. [God] has placed before you fire and water; stretch out your hand for whichever *you choose*" (Sirach 15:15–16).

Your word, O Lord, has called us continually to a fruitful way of life lived in you and in harmony with one another: "For as the rain and the snow come down from heaven, and do not return there until they have watered the earth, making it bring forth and sprout, giving seed to the sower and bread to the eater, so shall my word be that goes out from my mouth; it shall not return to me empty, but it shall accomplish *that which I purpose* [*desire*], and succeed in the thing for which I sent it" (Isaiah 55:10–11).

But the people rebelled and strayed, despite knowing what God wished for them, saying,
However, we resisted. You told us that "though your sins are like scarlet, they shall be like snow…If you *are willing* [*desiring*] and obedient, you shall eat the good of the land; but if you refuse [*do not desire*] and rebel, you shall be devoured by the sword" (Isaiah 1:18–20).

Neither threat nor plea sufficed to turn from clinging to our ways, rejecting yours. We pursued, rather, forgetfulness, deceit, rebellion, idolatry, and defiance.

Seeing the people's behavior, prophetic voices spoke on behalf of God:

> "They did not keep God's covenant, but refused [*did not wish*] to walk according to his law. They forgot what [God] had done…" ◆ PSALM 78:10–11

> Why has this people turned away in perpetual backsliding? Thy have held fast to deceit; they have *refused* [*not wished*] to return. ◆ JEREMIAH 8:5

> But they rebelled against me and would not [*wished not to*] *listen* to me; not one of them cast away the detestable things their eyes feasted on, nor did they forsake the idols of Egypt. ◆ EZEKIEL 20:8

> O Lord, do your eyes not look for truth? You have struck them, but they felt no anguish; you have consumed them, *but they refused* [*did not wish*] *to take correction*. They have made their faces harder than rock; they have refused to turn back. ◆ JEREMIAH 5:3

The people again replied,
Though sages taught us to discern between the *Two Paths*, we walked in our own ways. Though you promised, threatened, and cajoled that we listen to Torah and the counsels of the prophets, we defied you. And the vicious cycle of return-defy-return-defy continued. Still, we cling to the divine promise made through Ezekiel to us in exile:

> Therefore, say to the house of Israel, Thus says the Lord God: It is not for your sake, O house of Israel, that I am about to act, but for the sake of my holy name, which you have profaned among the nations to which you came. I will sanctify my great name, which has been profaned among the nations, and which you have profaned among them; and the nations shall know that I am the Lord, says the Lord God, when through you I display my holiness before their eyes. ⁌ EZEKIEL 36:22–23

God looked at the human heart and saw stone. Rather than threatening more destruction, the divine physician proposed to remove that boulder and replace it instead with a real heart, placing the Spirit within to help all walk the *Way to Life*!

> I will take you from the nations, and gather you from all the countries, and bring you into your own land.
>
> I will sprinkle clean water upon you, and you shall be clean from all your uncleannesses, and from all your idols I will cleanse you.
>
> A new heart I will give you, and a new spirit I will put within you; and I will remove from your body the heart of stone and give you a heart of flesh.

> I will put my spirit within you, and make you follow my statutes and be careful to observe my ordinances.
>
> ◦᠄ see EZEKIEL 36:21–31

God never severs the covenant, never walks away from the promises, made to Israel. Instead, he promises that God's spirit will come to them and they will be restored.

Summary and Segue

The Septuagint employed *thélo* to illustrate the clash of wills between Israel/Judah and their Redeemer. God asked for worship and for justice toward neighbors and the poor. The people wished to worship themselves, clinging desperately to their own desires. False worship (idolatry) and oppression of the poor were the very symptoms that elicited both prophetic censure *and* the promise of a new heart.

What did Mark take from Israel's treasure of teaching? How did the gospel view the human engagement with Christ? Willfulness? Obstinacy? Blindness? Let us now study how the second gospel diagnoses the human heart through the lens of the Greek *thélo*.

As we look into the mirror that is the Marcan portrayal of the disciples, perhaps we can catch a glimpse of *our* fundamental leanings. How will God fulfill the promises he has made in Jesus' ministry?

Thélo in the Gospel of Mark

The Marcan Jesus rushes onto the scene seemingly out of nowhere. Baptized by John. Confirmed by the Spirit: "You are my Beloved!" Tempted by the enemy. He cried out with dogged determination, "Repent, and believe in the good news!" And everyone around him reacts, exposing their deepest desires.

Jesus teaches the Good News and heals. Following several early cures, a leper comes to him begging, "If you *wish* (*thélo*), you can make me clean." Jesus proclaims *his* deepest desire, touches the leper, and says, "I do *so wish*. Be made clean!" (1:40–41). The leper goes away beloved, whole, restored to his family and village. However, because Jesus had touched the leper, he himself has to remain outside of towns since he had taken on the leper's uncleanness.

Next, after healing a paralytic, calling Levi to follow him, rebuffing the scribes and Pharisees several times, and healing many others, "he went up the mountain and called to him those whom he *wanted*....And he appointed twelve, whom he also named apostles, to be with him, and to be sent out to proclaim the message" (3:13–14).

Alarming signs of antagonism to the *Way* foreshadow Jesus' death. The malice of Herodias, illicit wife of Herod, comes to a head when she recognizes her chance to be done with John the Baptist: "Herodias *wished* to kill him...Herod said to the girl, 'Ask me for whatever you *wish* and I will give it...' 'I *want* you to give me at once the head of John the Baptist on a platter'" (see Mark 6:17–29). Willful and vengeful, Herodias wanted him dead. Herodias *wanted* John dead—no more opposition, no more prophetic challenge. Self-will? Defiance? Self-protection?

The gospel's use of *thélo* uncovers the *desires* of each of the players. Herodias wanted to have John silenced forever. No more troubling word from this wild man. As if to underscore his diagnosis of her tendencies, Jesus later replies to a question about the coming of the prophet Elijah:

> Elijah is indeed coming first to restore all things. How then is it written about the Son of Man, that he is to go through many sufferings and be treated with contempt? But I tell

you that Elijah has come, and they did to him whatever they [*wished*], as it is written about him. ▶ 9:12–13

Jesus, on the other hand, wanted to heal. He wanted twelve from among his disciples to bear the good news: "You are my Beloved!" The second gospel continues to diagnose the deeper intents of the human heart, to bring to light hidden motives so that the divine physician can heal all.

Thélo in the Context of Jesus' Instructing the Twelve *and* the Disciples

At the beginning of the gospel, Jesus sees Simon and Andrew "casting a net into the sea" (1:16ff). Mark's calculated use of the Greek verb *'amphibállo* resonates strongly with its sole occurrence in the Septuagint in the book of the prophet Habakkuk:

> Are you not from of old, O LORD my God, my Holy One?...You have made people like the fish of the sea, like crawling things that have no ruler. *The enemy* brings all of them up with a hook; *he drags them out with his net (*'amphibléstron*), he gathers them in his seine; so he rejoices and exults. Therefore he sacrifices to (*'amphibállo*) his net (*'amphibléstron*) and makes offerings to his seine; for by them his portion is lavish, and his food is rich.
> ▶ HABAKKUK 1:12–16

Thus, "casting a net" subtly identifies Simon and Andrew as blind idolaters needing repentance. What seals the deal on this interpretation is that Peter and Andrew left behind *diktúa*, real, physical nets, not nets of idolatry. Considering this, we might be startled: they left the wrong nets! Mark is telling us that they followed Jesus as idolaters who were clueless about their need for repentance. In many ways, they function as proxies for all other disciples—including us. We are often blind to what we drag behind us, to that which influences everything we say and do.

The disciples walk with him, always lugging their snares of iniquity behind them, blind to their drag. Between chapters eight and ten, we get to see how their interactions with Jesus disclose their precious self-absorption and wounded defensiveness. Jesus' teaching about the *Path to Life* exposes their resistance and their complicity with the *Path toward Death*.

It is important to underline how the disciples continue along with him, even in the face of painful disclosures. While highly attracted to him, they remain oblivious to the deeper implications of his Messiahship. Equally amazing, Jesus doesn't dismiss them. Neither do they change!

This first example of Mark's use of *thélo* regarding the disciples uncovers for us Peter's basic and unrecognized drive to gain the whole world. On the *way* (*hodós*) to Caesarea Phillipi, Jesus asked his disciples, "Who do people say that I am?" We know their responses. We remember how Peter named him "Messiah." To spell out the meaning of this, Jesus taught them he must suffer, be rejected by the elders, the chief priests, and scribes, be killed, and rise after three days. Peter rebuked him. Jesus did not pass over Peter's denial: "Get behind me, Satan! [Go behind me where disciples belong, you Tempter!] *For you are setting your mind not on divine things but on human things*" (see 8:33).

Why does Jesus call Peter "Satan"? Because Peter tempted Jesus to abandon his mission and destiny in the same way the tempter does in the desert. In Mark's gospel, *Satanás* refers to anyone who tempts Jesus to turn away from the *Path toward Life* and abandon his mission. What motivates Peter to resist? His own demand that Jesus reject what Peter fears: "Do not lose your life!"

Immediately, Jesus counters Peter's intervention by pointing to what desire looks like in the Reign of God. He calls his disciples to examine their inclinations along the way.

> He called the crowd with his disciples, and said to them, "If any *want* (*thélo*) to become my followers, let them deny themselves and take up their cross and follow me. For those who *want* to save their life will lose it, and those who lose their life for my sake, and for the sake of the gospel, will save it. For what will it profit them to gain the whole world and forfeit their life?" 8:34–36

Hard words. Easy to dismiss. Astoundingly, Peter and his cohort still walk behind him even though unwilling to accept his word. The vision of the Reign of God to which Jesus calls them lies so far outside their comfort zone they can't see it. Their desire to gain the whole world, to have everything that would answer every need and guarantee their security, renders them obstinate.

Next, Jesus comes down the mountain of Transfiguration with James, John, and Peter, from an event that had revealed their fear and desire to domesticate Jesus. The episode uncovered their unconscious ambition (*thélo*) to gain the whole world by confining him snugly in a booth with Moses and Elijah nearby.

Immediately, they meet a child with a spirit that rendered him deaf and mute. The other disciples had failed to cast it out, for "this kind can come out only through prayer" (9:29). The child's deaf and mute spirit mirrors their own situation, since prayer had yet to open *their* hearts to "wanting to lose their lives for the sake of the gospel." They could not even begin to entertain Jesus' teaching about *wanting* to be his followers.

Jesus' second prediction of his passion followed directly. His disciples, deaf and mute themselves, implicitly reveal their desire to gain the whole world by their mute deafness. They just could not take in his words: "But they did not understand what he was saying and were afraid to ask him" (9:32). They didn't want to take up their crosses or lose their lives for Jesus' sake. Their resistance shows itself as not hearing and *not wanting* to talk about it.

Together in the house in Capernaum, Jesus broaches the subject of their "arguing...*on the way*." They had been quarreling about who is the greatest, about who would gain more of the world than the others. Seizing the moment, he teaches the Twelve, saying, "Whoever *wants* to be first must be last of all and servant of all" (see 9:33–37). What a challenging word!

John changes the subject at once, announcing how he upheld the honor of the Jesus-clan by preventing another from casting out demons. Jesus replies: "Do not stop him...Whoever is not against us is for us" (9:38–40). Taking it further, Jesus adds, "If your hand causes you to stumble, cut it off...If your foot causes you to stumble, cut it off...and if your eye..." (9:42–47). The divine physician recommends radical surgery for their lust for power, prestige, and control. Yikes!

Not long after, a rich man seeks affirmation from Jesus for his attempts to gain eternal life. He becomes mortified by the response: "'You lack one thing; go, sell what you own, and give the money to the poor, and you will have treasure in heaven; then come, follow me.' When he heard, he was shocked and went away grieving, for he had many possessions" (10:17–22). Jesus drives home his point about gaining the whole world: "It is easier for a camel to go through the eye of a needle than for someone who is rich to enter the kingdom of God." The disciples suddenly find their voice, crying out, "Then who can be saved?"

Peter bargains, "Look, we have left everything and followed you..." Jesus replies, "[you] will...receive a hundredfold now in this age—houses, brothers and sisters, mothers and children, and fields, with persecutions—and in the age to come eternal life. *But many who are first will be last, and the last will be first"* (10:28–31). Not all that consoling, eh?

With this word, Jesus moves on. "They were on the *way*, going up to Jerusalem, and Jesus was walking ahead of them; they were amazed (*astounded; alarmed; terror-struck; insolent*), and those who followed were afraid." He took the twelve aside and again told them of his passion and death (10:32).

Their desire to gain the whole world could not be contained: James and John want to settle who was first and who was last by going to the source. "'Teacher, we *want* (*thélo*) you to do for us whatever we ask of you.' And he said to them, 'What is it you *want* me to do for you?'...'Grant us to sit, one at your right hand and one at your left in your glory.'" We know Jesus' reply about drinking the cup he would drink (10:35–40). Predictable sibling rivalry flares immediately! "When the ten heard this, they began to be angry with James and John." Who's number one!

Recognizing potential mutiny as a teachable moment, Jesus counsels them, saying:

> among the Gentiles those whom they recognize as their rulers lord it over them, and their great ones are tyrants over them. But it is not so among you; but whoever *wishes* (*thélo*) to become great among you must be your servant, and whoever *wishes* to be first among you must be slave of all. For the Son of Man came not to be served but to serve... 🔊 10:41–45

Summary so far: The two paths diverge early in the gospel. By studying the verb *thélo*, we see how Mark illustrates the *Path toward Life* in the episode with the leper from chapter one. A leper begs, "If you wish, you can make me clean." "I do wish. Be made clean!" The leper clearly sees he needs healing from disease, resentment at being considered unworthy, fear of being treated as damaged goods, envy at others' good fortune, unbearable insecurity, profound loneliness, and more. Seeing his plight, he begs.

In chapter six, Mark's portrayal of the malice of Herodias shows us the *Path to Death*. Herodias *wished* to kill John. Herod said to his daughter, "'Ask me for whatever you *wish*, and I will give it…' 'I *want* you to give me at once the head of John the Baptist on a platter.'" Willful and vengeful, Herodias wanted him dead. Blind to her malice, she had John killed (6:17–29).

The disciples and the Twelve are blind to the *Path to Life* and react forcefully to Jesus' teaching. They wish nothing to do with Jesus' mission or teaching. Denying self and losing self and giving up possessions make no sense at all. Thus, they sit at the crossroads with Bartimaeus, familiar with the *Path toward Death* and enamored of riches, prestige, ambition, dominance, and power. Which way will these unseeing disciples follow?

The very next event Mark records is the healing of the blind beggar Bartimaeus, the perfect foil for disciples. Many in the crowd, including disciples, attempted to squelch his cry for mercy, possibly reacting to Jesus' teaching about being the slave of all. The blind beggar throws off his cloak, giving up all he had (as different from the rich man above), and comes to Jesus.

Here, Mark deals with the heart of discipleship: "What do you *want* me to do for you?" (Jesus had posed the same question to James and John above.) And the blind man replies, "My teacher, let me see again" [literally, "that I may look up!"]. Jesus tells him to go forth; his faith had saved him. And the formerly blind beggar who, at the beginning of this passage was sitting at the crossroads between the two ways, begins to walk the *Way to Life* behind Jesus. Seeing his situation clearly, he asks; Jesus heals/saves; he looks up, *sees, and follows* (10:46–52). Bartimaeus is the only one to this point in Mark's gospel who sees and follows.

QUESTIONS TO BRING TO YOUR PRAYER

1. The people of Israel know what God wants of them, yet they continuously wander from the path to which he has called them.
   - What do you think causes human beings to act against what we know is right?
   - How well are we—and you—doing with this challenge today?
   - What dramas tend to follow acting contrary to our best intentions?

2. What do you think of the idea of there being a clash of wills between God and humanity?
   - What fuels our obstinance?
   - What causes our blindness?

3. Christ teaches the gospel to deaf, blind, and invincibly ignorant disciples. One day, they will bear much fruit even as they go on the way in a state of fear, doubt, and disbelief. This is discipleship. Just like them, we don't clean up our acts first.
   - So, do you recognize their path as yours—resistant, deaf, blind?
   - Might you wish to wait until you clean up your act before presenting yourself as a disciple? If so, what's behind that?

4. Whatever we see, we can bring to the Light; God alone can thaw our hearts.
   - What places of resistance in you need healing?

Chapter Five

THE WAY TOWARD DEATH—SCRIBES AND PHARISEES

When we set ourselves to change ourselves or others,
we do so out of intolerance...
We cannot bear with a shortcoming,
a defect, a moral or psychological weakness in ourselves,
and we set about correcting it
with hidden spite and ill-concealed violence.

We seek to change in order to be accepted,
to conform to expectations,
to live up to the ideal image
we have made up for ourselves.
We are impatient with ourselves,
and so we want to force ourselves to change...

No growth results from violence...
The paradox of change
is that it is only by forgetting it
that it can ever take place, if it does at all.
Resistance to ourselves,
to anything in ourselves,
only serves to strengthen
that which we are resisting,
and thus makes change impossible.[8]
   CARLOS G. VALLES, SJ, *MASTERING SADHANA*

Origins and Program of the Pharisees

The Pharisees have always reminded me of "those" grade school kids who tattled on classmates to Sr. Mortimer to ensure order and guarantee the wrongdoers were punished. It has been easy for me to write the Pharisees off as "those whiny, self-righteous prigs who didn't like Jesus." However, recent studies into the first-century Jewish world of Jesus have shed new light upon their setting and life.

Two centuries after Cyrus of Persia allowed Judean exiles to return to Jerusalem from Babylon, Alexander the Great and his successors imposed Greek culture upon the Middle East

---

8 Carlos G. Valles, SJ, *Mastering Sadhana: On Retreat with Anthony de Mello* (New York: Image Books/Doubleday, 1988).

(332 BCE). The Pharisees' separatist reform movement opposed attempts to Hellenize the Jewish population—a social agenda that was supported by the Sadducees. The Pharisees helped Jews safeguard Jewish identity and live religiously in a world replete with the allure of pagan ways by promoting close observance of purity laws. The several books of Maccabees tell the story of the brothers Maccabees and how they revolted over Greek impositions, overthrew Antiochus IV Epiphanes, and established a monarchy that ensured the nation's sovereignty for a century (164–63 BCE).

During the occupation by Rome and the reign of King Herod (post-63 BCE), different schools of thought developed within the Pharisee movement. The famous rabbi Hillel taught a rather gentle approach to Torah, especially regarding purity laws. Rabbi Shammai promoted a more rigorous approach—again, to sustain Jewish identity in a hostile world. Jesus appears to have clashed with the followers of Shammai over the following principles.

God promised the land to the Chosen People. Roman occupation threatened their divinely appointed inheritance—the thing that most firmly attested to the fidelity of God. Family and land provided refuge in a hostile world. So when Jesus called disciples to follow him, he drew them from the security of family and land toward trust in God alone. Insecurity, anyone?

Shammai promoted avoidance of whomever was deemed unclean—Gentiles, sinners, lepers, women with a flow of blood. Yet, whom did Jesus touch and heal? With whom did he break bread? Hmmm.

Shammai prohibited any work on the Sabbath. Jesus defended his disciples against the Pharisees for plucking grain on the Sabbath, declaring, "The Son of Man is lord even of the sabbath" (Mark 2:28). Blasphemy?

The Pharisees esteemed the Temple as the most potent sign of religious and national identity, the place from which instruction, mercy, and forgiveness of sins flowed. Yet Jesus taught, forgave sins, healed, and promoted a non-nationalistic identity for his followers in the Reign of God.

And when Jesus cleansed the Temple (11:15–18), told the parable of the wicked tenants (12:1–12), and foretold the destruction of the Temple (13:1–8), he announced the presence of the Messiah and the arrival of the Reign of God. Nationalist symbols of security and identity were undone. Are we surprised the Pharisees (and the scribes) opposed him at every turn? Let's see how the second gospel portrays them.

Scribes and Pharisees—Early Skirmishes

The non-violent followers of Gandhi and Martin Luther King Jr. received the violence of those who opposed them *so that the violent might be confounded by their violence and repent*. Two thousand years before them, Jesus summoned everyone to repentance and elicited deep-seated reactions from each and every one *so all might recognize their resistance and bring it to the Light*. It is true today. Seeing how aggressively hostile we in mainstream America have become *could* open our eyes and turn our hearts.

Jesus' encounters with the scribes and Pharisees illustrate this dynamic well. He shone his light on their *Path toward Death* and drew to the surface their self-will and aggressive self-defense. Except for one scribe, all remained blind to the trajectory of their actions.

It is important to note that there is not one, generic gospel. Mark is not Matthew is not Luke is certainly not John. We will investigate Mark's understanding of opposition to Jesus by paying close attention to his interactions with the scribes and Pharisees. We will study Mark's use of *thélo* within the context of the entire gospel. Our part? Let us consider the scribes and Pharisees as a foil for disciples of Jesus both *then* and *now*. They reveal to us the very "stuff" we don't want to see and yet have to deal with every day.

We begin by recalling Jesus' baptism, temptation in the wilderness, and his initial message (1:9ff): "The time is fulfilled, and the kingdom of God has come near; repent, and believe in the good news!" (1:14f). He calls others to affiliate themselves with a new clan grounded in the good news: "You are my…Beloved!" (1:11). Repent and believe! Interestingly enough, his early deeds cause nary a stir.

Soon, locals witness Jesus' teaching-with-authority (*unlike the scribes!*) and his healing of the person with an unclean spirit (1:21ff). Next, he heals Simon's mother-in-law, and quickly crowds gather seeking to be cured (1:29ff). Experiencing the power of Jesus the healer, the people begin to broadcast the news about him. Jesus leaves Capernaum to preach in Galilee, casting out even more demons (1:34ff). And, even though Jesus' healing touch of a leper rendered Jesus unclean and unfit to move about freely under the precepts of the law, people still come to him in droves (1:40ff).

Suddenly, the scribes appear. They scrutinize him (2:1ff). They seethe when he forgives the sins of the paralytic lowered through the roof: "It is blasphemy! Who can forgive sins but God alone?" Jesus not only cures the paralytic; he proclaims his authority to forgive sins. The sight of the paralytic walking out the door mat-in-hand amazes the people and mortifies the scribes.

In the wake of Jesus' actions, the outraged scribes and the Pharisees dog his steps. Jesus continues to break the rules, calling Levi and enjoying a grand party with outcasts. The scribes and Pharisees protest, "Why does he eat with tax collectors and sinners?" Jesus prods them: "I have come to call not the righteous but sinners" (2:13ff). "He is unclean!" they were surely thinking. The Pharisees then materialize to critique his disciples: "Why are they picking grain on the Sabbath?" Jesus humiliates them. He makes the outrageous claim to be lord of the Sabbath! (2:23ff). "Blasphemy!"

The Spirit who descends upon Jesus at his baptism drives him to proclaim repentance and good news: "You are God's beloved! Accept your true identity!" Why are the scribes and Pharisees blind and deaf? What do they cling to?

Scribes and Pharisees—Growing Hostility

But the mystery of iniquity is
that I may easily and without infringing
on any commandment
but rather allowing myself to be
a decent average representative of my society,
make it be the case
that I do not have a heart to give.

Scripture refers to the hardness of heart…
the subtler point is
that the heart as such cannot be hard.
It can only be suppressed or,
to change the metaphor, encased.
We get so used to regarding the hard heart
as the source of evil actions,
that we become incapable of seeing
that the hard heart is the evil person's victim.

 DOM SEBASTIAN MOORE, OSB,
THE CRUCIFIED JESUS IS NO STRANGER, P. 76

Jesus goes to the synagogue on the Sabbath. A man with a withered hand rises. The scribes and Pharisees watch his every move. Jesus tests them. They reveal their hardened hearts.

> Then he said to them, "Is it lawful to do good or to do harm on the sabbath, to save life or to kill?" But they were silent. He looked around at them with anger; he was grieved at their hardness of heart and said to the man, "Stretch out your hand." He stretched it out, and his hand was restored. The Pharisees went out and immediately conspired with the Herodians against him, how to destroy him. 🔊 3:4–6

Destroy him? Fear of losing supremacy drives them to plot with those who killed the Baptizer. Their urgency to destroy Jesus relates exactly to the earlier response of the unclean spirit, "Have you come here to destroy us?" Jesus the Physician exposes their encased hearts not to shame them, but to open their eyes to their violence because they are *"Beloved of God."*

Very soon afterwards, the scribes from Jerusalem act to sabotage Jesus' authority, accusing him of conniving with Beelzebul. Projection? As you may recall, he beat them at their own game, disrespecting them before the crowds.

> "Truly I tell you, people will be forgiven for their sins and whatever blasphemies they utter; but whoever blasphemes against the Holy Spirit can never have forgiveness, but is guilty of an eternal sin"—for they had said, "He has an unclean spirit." 🔊 3:28–30

The scribes and Pharisees spy on Jesus' disciples. Aha! They do not wash their hands before eating. They disobey the traditions of the elders! Jesus turned the tables on them, denouncing *them* for abandoning the commands of God by holding to human traditions. "Hypocrites!"

> He said to them, "Isaiah prophesied rightly about you hypocrites, as it is written, 'This people honors me with their lips, but their hearts are far from me; in vain do they worship me, teaching human precepts as doctrines.'"
> ◁ 7:6–7

Jesus openly opposes their stance on purity laws. "Whatever goes into a person from outside cannot defile…It is what comes out of a person that defiles!" This is key: Their habitual aversion to introspection keeps them blind, even though he lays bare the reality of the underlying hardness of their hearts:

> "For it is from within, from the human heart, that evil intentions come: fornication, theft, *murder*, adultery, avarice, wickedness, deceit, licentiousness, envy, slander, pride, folly. All these evil things come from within, and they defile a person." ◁ 7:21–23

In a flurry of activity, Jesus heals the daughter of a Syrophoenician woman ("even the dogs under the table eat the children's crumbs"; see 7:24–30). He travels to the region of the Decapolis and heals a man who was deaf and mute (7:31–37). He feeds a crowd of four thousand with seven loaves and immediately goes with his disciples to the district of Dalmanutha (8:1–10). Here the Pharisees seek a sign. He replies, "No sign will be given to this generation." Then, after having just provided a sign (!), he gets into the boat again (8:11–13).

During the crossing, he warns his disciples: "Beware of [rather, *see (blépo)*] the yeast of the Pharisees and the yeast of Herod." Recognize it in yourselves! Duh.

> They said to one another, "It is because we have no bread."

> And becoming aware of it, Jesus said to them, *"Why are you talking about having no bread? Do you still not perceive or understand? Are your hearts hardened? Do you have eyes, and fail to see? Do you have ears, and fail to hear? And do you not remember? When I broke the five loaves for the five thousand, how many baskets full of broken pieces did you collect?"...Then he said to them, "Do you not yet understand?"* 8:16–21

As Jesus brings into the light the invincible ignorance and hardness of heart of the deaf, blind, and forgetful disciples *so they might see*, Mark identifies them with the scribes and Pharisees who are also blind, deaf, and mute—all of these people have hardened their hearts and go along maintaining benign views of themselves. Each walks blindly the *Path toward Death*.

Following this dust-up with the disciples, Jesus cures a blind person at Bethsaida in a two-step process (8:22–26). It demonstrates his intent to heal *all* from blindness—the Twelve, the disciples, the scribes and Pharisees, and us. Indeed, Jesus desires to heal. *Yet, none of these ever recognizes their blindness and asks to see!*

Peter's crucial confession follows: "You are the Messiah." Jesus rebukes Peter, saying, "Get behind me, Satan! For you are setting your mind not on divine things but on human things" (8:31–33). This saying leads to the following crucial teaching, *to which all were blind, notably the scribes and Pharisees*:

> He called the crowd with his disciples, and said to them, "If any *want* to become my followers, let them deny themselves and take up their cross and follow me. For those who *want* to save their life will lose it, and those who lose their life for my sake, and for the sake of the gospel, will save it." MARK 8:34–35

Unable to recognize their true situation and seek healing, they reject this word.

Scribes, Pharisees, and Chief Priests—Murderous Intent
Some Pharisees confront Jesus in Judea beyond the Jordan to trap him: "Is it lawful for a man to divorce his wife?" He parries their attack (10:1–9). Exeunt Pharisees. When, after he blesses the little children, whom the disciples snub, and challenges the rich man to "sell what you own, give the money to the poor…then come, follow me," he reiterates his coming rejection.

> They were on the road, going up to Jerusalem, and *Jesus was walking ahead of them; they were amazed, and those who followed were afraid.* He took the twelve aside again and began to tell them what was to happen to him, saying, "See, we are going up to Jerusalem, and *the Son of Man will be handed over to the chief priests and the scribes*, and they will condemn him to death…" 10:32–33

Notice that Mark does not implicate the Pharisees in Jesus' rejection, trial, crucifixion, and death. Though their hard-hearted opposition and contempt rivaled that of the scribes, for some reason they step off the trajectory toward death. Still, their resolute blindness to his person and mission differs little from that of the disciples and the Twelve.

Immediately thereafter, James and John request to sit at Jesus' right and left in his glory.

> James and John, the sons of Zebedee, came forward to him and said to him, "Teacher, *we want (thélo)* you to do for us whatever we ask of you." And he said to them, "*What is it you want (thélo)* me to do for you?" And they said to him,

"Grant us to sit, one at your right hand and one at your left, in your glory…" 🔊 10:35FF

"But it is not so among you; but *whoever wishes* (*thélo*) to become great among you must be your servant, and *whoever wishes* (*thélo*) to be first among you must be slave of all." 🔊 10:43F

It is simple and straightforward. James and John seek personal honor and power. Jesus calls them from that path to self-emptying charity. Still, James, John, and the other disciples remain blind, deaf, and dull to his teaching here and until the bitter end. Really. Perhaps we can sit there with Bartimaeus in that uncomfortable place and ask to look up.

The Continued Challenge by Jesus: Choose the Path of Life

Jesus does not relent in the face of the challenges issued especially by the scribes and Pharisees. With several stunningly provocative gestures, Jesus throws down the gauntlet at the feet of the religious authorities.

First, his regal entry into Jerusalem threatens their ascendancy—"Blessed is the coming kingdom of our ancestor David!" The people explicitly announce the arrival of the king and the end of their regime of fear and arrogance, vengeance and lies (11:1–11). Next, he cleanses the temple and puts its officials on notice that their circumscribed nationalistic identity has reached its end: "My house shall be called a house of prayer for all the nations. But you have made it a den of robbers" (11:15–17). Publicly disgraced, the scribes and chief priests ramp up their intent to make an end of this nuisance:

> And when the chief priests and the scribes heard it, they kept looking for a way [*how*] to kill him; for they were afraid of him, because the whole crowd was spellbound by his teaching. 🔊 11:18

Game on. The chief priests, scribes, and elders push harder: "By what authority are you doing these things?" He turns the tables on them yet again, asking, "Did the baptism of John come from heaven or was it of human origin?" Out of fear of the crowd, they resist answering. "We do not know." And Jesus shames them: "Neither will I tell you by what authority I am doing these things" (11:27–33). Jesus seeks to expose their intentions *so they might see themselves and turn toward the Path to Life*.

We know the parable of the wicked tenants (Mark 12:1–12). The owner let out his vineyard to tenants. When he sent slaves to collect produce, they seize them, beat them, and send them away empty-handed. Finally, he sent his son. "This is the heir; come, let us kill him, and the inheritance will be ours!" He unmasks their demand for dominance. Jesus leans in, saying,

> "Have you not read this scripture: 'The stone that the builders rejected has become the cornerstone; this was the Lord's doing, and it is amazing in our eyes'?" When they realized that he had told this parable against them, they wanted to arrest him, but they feared the crowd.
> 🔊 12:10–12

They remain radically blind to their entitlement, possessiveness, and claims to sovereignty. They are as sightless as Bartimaeus.

The chief priests, the scribes, and the elders attempt to outmaneuver Jesus by assigning Pharisees and Herodians to trap him into offending Rome: "Is it lawful to pay taxes to the emperor, or not?" Jesus sent them packing with a word: "Give to the emperor the things that are the emperor's, and to God the things that are God's" (12:13–17).

Jesus turns the tables and harasses the scribes—to the delight of the crowd. He poses a riddle about David naming Messiah both son and Lord. Not letting up, Jesus denounces the scribes, humiliating them by uncovering their game. They are all about appearances. Though he lifts the veil from their eyes, they refuse to recognize how Jesus threatens their security, prestige, reputation, status, and willful demands to be in charge. They remain blind to their hostility.

Then he teaches:

> As he taught, [Jesus] said, "Beware of the scribes, who *like* (*thélo*) to walk around in long robes, and to be greeted with respect in the marketplaces, and to have the best seats in the synagogues and places of honor at banquets! They *devour* widows' houses and for the sake of appearance say long prayers. They will receive the greater condemnation."
> 🔊 12:38–40

Why are long robes significant? They demonstrate the flagrant arrogance of the scribes. The Greek is *stólé*, vestments set aside for ministering in the Holy of Holies (see Exodus 28:2–4 and Leviticus 6:11 and *varia*). Mark skillfully connects their choice of dress with their blatant preening and need for adoration:

> Then Aaron shall lay both his hands on the head of the live goat, and confess over it all the iniquities of the people of Israel…and sending it away into the wilderness…He shall bathe his body in water in a holy place, and *put on his vestments*; then he shall come out and offer his burnt offering

and the burnt offering of the people, making atonement for himself and for the people. ▰ LEVITICUS 16:21–24

What wounds would drive them to parade publicly in vestments fit for the Holy of Holies? To seek respect in the market places? To claim the best seats in the synagogues? To be first in line at the wedding buffet? What do they protect? Inferiority? A desire to prove themselves better than others? Emptiness and the urge to impress others? Envy? Entitlement? Resentment of the temple priests in whose shadow they operated? As blind to their wounds as they are, so do they make Jesus pay the price for their unwillingness to look inside.

Another term worth noting is the verb *katesthío*, "to devour." Mark used it earlier in the gospel: "And as he sowed, some seed fell on the path, and the birds came and ate it up" (4:4). In a more startling connection, LXX used *katesthío* when describing the plague of locusts Moses called down upon Pharaoh. They devoured everything! That's what unrecognized hunger for prestige still fuels in our time.

> They shall *devour* the last remnant left you after the hail, and they shall *devour* every tree of yours that grows in the field…they *ate* all the plants in the land and all the fruit of the trees that the hail had left; nothing green was left, no tree, no plant in the field, in all the land of Egypt.
> ▰ EXODUS 10:5–15

This passage from Exodus adds further nuance to the traditional interpretation of the poor widow's grand act of putting two small copper coins into the temple treasure (Mark 12:41–44). He indicts the scribes for ravaging the houses of poor widows (like locusts!) while withholding their own treasure.

"Truly I tell you, this poor widow has put in more than all those who are contributing to the treasury. *For all of them have contributed out of their abundance*; but she out of her poverty has put in everything she had, all she had to live on." 12:43–44

Scribes and Chief Priests and Elders—The End Game

But the words of her elder son Esau
were told to Rebekah;
so she sent and called her younger son Jacob
and said to him,
"Your brother Esau is consoling himself
by planning to kill you." GENESIS 27:42

The gospel writer straightaway makes known the cunning and deadly intent of the scribes and chief priests who fear Rome's intervention and the end of their sovereignty.

> It was two days before the Passover and the festival of Unleavened Bread. The chief priests and the scribes were looking for a way to arrest Jesus by stealth and kill him; for they said, "Not during the festival, or there may be a riot among the people." 14:1–2

One of the Twelve, Judas Iscariot, walks farther down the *Path toward Death* directly to the door of the chief priests. They plot to seize Jesus at night (14:10–11). Judas leads an armed mob from the chief priests, scribes, and elders to Gethsemane to arrest his rabbi (14:43–50).

The high priest with the chief priests, elders, and scribes entertain false witnesses against Jesus, accusing him of conspiracy to destroy the Temple. Frustrated, the high priest asks Jesus whether he is the Messiah. He answers, "I am; and 'you shall see the Son of Man seated at the right hand of the Power' and 'coming with the clouds of heaven'" (see Daniel 7:13). "Blasphemy!" They nailed him (14:53–65).

Mark shows us Peter walking the *Path toward Death*. He denies any connection with Jesus, swearing, "I do not know the man!" Yet Peter, precisely in the heat of denial, *remembers*, sees himself clearly, breaks down, weeps, and suddenly finds the *Way to Life* (14:66–72). Memory of Jesus' words opens his eyes and heart! He recognizes his plight. Tears cleanse his self-idolatry.

The chief priests, elders, scribes, and the entire council conspire (15:1). They revise their "religious" charge of blasphemy into something to catch Pilate's attention—treason and sedition: "Are you the King of the Jews?" Pilate recognizes their jealousy. They meet his attempt to release the King of the Jews with malice. "Crucify him!" He releases Barabbas, a murderer, into the custody of murderers (15:6–15).

The scribes and the chief priests mock Jesus crucified: "He saved others; he cannot save himself. Let the Messiah, the King of Israel, come down from the cross now, so that we may see and believe" (15:31f). Mark's final depiction of the scribes and chief priests thus reveals their encased hearts and murderous victory.

They achieved their endgame, his death, demonstrating, then and for all time, murder as the aim of *all* self-absorbed defense against the intrusion of the *Way to Life*. The human condition? Indeed, it's the condition *from which* Jesus summoned all to turn from and follow him then—and now.

Bartimaeus: Illuminating the Path for All Who Cannot See
In all these incidents in Mark, we see a fundamental problem: everyone in the gospel of Mark believes he or she can see. Yet when

Jesus encroaches on their turf, most react defiantly. Except those healed. Yet none of them, save Bartimaeus, sees *and* follows Jesus. Not the scribes and Pharisees, not the disciples who are alongside him, not those who are seeking out his healing. And so we return to Bartimaeus, the blind one sitting on the way. Unlike all those who have come before him, Bartimaeus, the one who begs to see, not only is restored to sight but is empowered to follow Jesus on the *Way to Life* (10:46–52). What is unique to this story?

I have come to believe that Mark identifies a process basic to discipleship here. Bartimaeus, unlike most others who interact with Jesus in this gospel, is aware of his blindness *and* poverty. Absolutely clear about his situation—his disability, that which has put him at the crossroads—Bartimaeus begs to see. Jesus heals him. And Bartimaeus is transformed. And Bartimaeus follows Jesus.

The process has four simple steps:

Awareness » *bold request* » *seeing clearly Jesus' mission and teaching* » *discipleship*

None of the Twelve, the disciples, scribes, or Pharisees are willing or able to take an honest look at themselves and their own vulnerability. So they do not ask anything of Jesus that could possibly open the Reign of God to them. None are aware enough to make the bold request that will lead them to true sight and the ability to be true disciples of Jesus. We like to think that we are just like the disciples; it may be that we are like the scribes and Pharisees, as well.

If we allow it, we can begin to recognize our own woundedness. We might even see it in the ways in which our woundedness plays out in how we treat others. Perhaps in seeing our own poor plight, like Bartimaeus, we might beg to see, to follow, and to know, "You are my Beloved!"

QUESTIONS TO BRING TO YOUR PRAYER

1. What do you notice about the scribes and Pharisees?
   - Can you describe the trajectory of their resistance to Jesus?
   - Why did it result in murder? In what ways do they represent the way toward death?
   - Why is it so easy to see scribes and Pharisees today out there and not in the mirror?

2. They were unwilling to take the first step of honestly naming their blindness.
   - Why is this so difficult?

3. With what character in these many incidents in Mark do you most closely identify?
   - Why?
   - Who brings out the strongest reaction in you?
   - Why?

Chapter Six

FIVE INFIRM ON THE WAY

We hold a treasure not made of gold
In earthen vessels, wealth untold
One treasure only, the Lord, the Christ
In earthen vessels.
🔊 **JOHN B. FOLEY, SJ,** *EARTHEN VESSELS*
from the collection of the same name

Jesus preached what he had heard at his baptism: "You are my Beloved" (Mark 1:11). Burdened, wounded people came to him seeking freedom from their diseases. His healing word and touch cured them. They heard the good news and realized, perhaps for the first time, they were indeed beloved of God. They admitted their struggles and begged for healing.

How is it, then, that scribes, Pharisees, and disciples respond with resistance and antagonism? It seems to me that they staunchly refuse to recognize how their response to Jesus stems directly from their wounds. They remain blind to what fuels their opposition to Jesus' mission. Whether we resist his message passionately or simply brush it off, something we often don't see—something we are blind to—impels us.

Let us consider five encounters of healing. In each, a person realizes his or her need. What did each see that allows them to open outward? Notice that in each of these stories, the person being healed serves as a foil to the aversions of scribes, Pharisees, disciples, and the Twelve—and ourselves.

Unclean Spirits and the Words that Describe Them

At the very start of the Gospel of Mark, we find Jesus teaching in the synagogue at Capernaum (Mark 1:21–28). Hearing him, all were *amazed* (*ekplesso*) at his authoritative teaching. There is a man in the synagogue who is plagued by an unclean spirit. He is aggressive and defiant: "What have you to do with us, Jesus of Nazareth? Have you come to destroy (*apóllumi*) us? I know who you are, the Holy One of God!" (1:24). Jesus rebukes the spirit and commands it to come out.

Watching this episode, the people are *amazed*, but in a different way. But our English translation again falls short: this time they are not *ekplesso*; they are *thambéo* (alarmed, terror-struck). It's the sort of alarm the disciples express later when confronted with Jesus' teaching:

> "It is easier for a camel to go through the eye of a needle than for someone who is rich to enter the kingdom of God." *They were greatly astounded and said to one another,* "Then who can be saved?" ❧ 10:25–26

They were on the way, going up to Jerusalem, and Jesus was
walking ahead of them; *they were amazed [astounded]*, and
those who followed were afraid... 10:32

Just as Jesus rebukes the man with the unclean spirit in the synagogue, so he will later rebuke Peter-*satanás*, who is possessed
by thinking human thoughts rather than divine thoughts. "Get
behind me..." (see 8:32f). Jesus, the divine physician, prescribes
the dying that leads to life in contrast to the vicious opposition
of the chief priests and scribes.

For those who *want to save their life will lose [apóllumi] it*,
and *those who lose [apóllumi] their life* for my sake, and for
the sake of the gospel, will save it. 8:35

And when the chief priests and the scribes heard it, *they
kept looking for a way to kill [destroy] him (apóllumi)*; for
they were afraid of him, because the whole crowd was
spellbound by his teaching. 11:18

We encounter unclean spirits for a second time when Jesus
arrives in the country of the Gerasenes. He immediately draws a
tormented man out from among the tombs (5:1–20). Isaiah refers
to such people as rebellious, self-willed idolaters who perform
sacrilegious rites among tombs (*mnéma*) amidst the dead (Isaiah
65:2–4). They are profoundly unclean. And yet the tomb is not
the final reality, don't we know. Ezekiel affirms it as a place of
rebirth.

"Thus says the Lord GOD: *I am going to open your graves, and
bring you up from your graves, O my people*; and I will bring
you back to the land of Israel..." EZEKIEL 37:12

The tormented man is uncontrollable, defying *restraint* (*déo*). Murderous perhaps? Mark uses this particular word (*déo*) to link him with the murderer Barabbas on the one hand and with Jesus' saving mission on the other.

> Now a man called Barabbas was in prison [*restrained* (*déo*)] with the rebels who had committed murder during the insurrection. 15:7

> I am the LORD, I have called you in righteousness, I have taken you by the hand and kept you; I have given you as a covenant to the people, a light to the nations, to open the eyes that are blind, *to bring out the prisoners* [*restrained* (*déo*)] *from the dungeon*, from the prison those who sit in darkness.
> ISAIAH 42:6–7

The unclean spirit Legion howls and cries out (*krázo*) in Jesus' presence (5:7; see 3:11). Again, there is foreshadowing of events to come when the crowd, stirred up by the chief priests' bloody intent, will also cry out in defiance of God:

> *They shouted back* (*krázo*), "Crucify him!" Pilate asked them, "Why, what evil has he done?" *But they shouted* all the more, "Crucify him!" MARK 15:13

However, this word also has a positive meaning when we look to the Septuagint. The word *krázo* is used in the Psalms to describe plaintive, even desperate, calling out to God:

> I sink in deep mire, where there is no foothold; I have come into deep waters, and the flood sweeps over me.

> *I am weary with my crying*; my throat is parched. My eyes grow dim with waiting for my God. 🔊 PSALM 69:2–3

> *Out of the depths I cry to you*, O LORD. Lord, hear my voice! Let your ears be attentive to the voice of my supplications!
> 🔊 PSALM 130:1–2

But even though Legion cries out (*krázo*), he does not want Jesus to intervene:

> "What have you to do with me, Jesus, Son of the Most High God? I adjure you by God, do not *torment* (*basanízo*) me." For he had said to him, "Come out of the man, you unclean spirit!"…"My name is Legion; for we are many."
> 🔊 MARK 5:7–9

The verb *basanízo*, "to torment," reveals Legion's aversion to Jesus' word of freedom. He fears the remedy more than his suffering. Sirach, once again a voice from the Wisdom literature of Israel, tells us what kind of torment Legion fears—the painful path to wisdom:

> For at first she [Wisdom] will walk with them on tortuous paths; she will bring fear and dread upon them, *and will torment them* (*basanízo*) *by her discipline* until she trusts them, and she will test them with her ordinances. Then she will come straight back to them again and gladden them, and will reveal her secrets to them. 🔊 SIRACH 4:17–18

Legion, in spite of its despair, feels threatened in its comfort zone by Jesus' words. In response, Legion reveals its capacity for self-annihilation when it goes out and kills a herd of pigs. In sum, the possessed man's actions portray for us the tortured inner lives of disciples, chief priests, scribes, and Pharisees (whose major revulsion was uncleanness). They receive Jesus' authoritative teaching ("Repent! You are Beloved!") as an attack against their well-defended worlds, and, fearing destruction, they too resist and threaten.

Let's continue to notice how we deal with threat. What fuels our fear and anger? What do we protect? What wounds can we bring to the Light?

The Leper
We meditate now on another event at the beginning of Mark's gospel: the leper healed by Jesus. Unlike the unclean spirits who opposed Jesus when he intrudes on their turf, the leper kneels and begs to be made clean (1:40–45). She knows her condition. She has been required to warn others of it daily: "Stay away! Unclean! Don't come near me!" She has learned to see herself as defiled, shamed, even damned.

Mark appears to comment on her situation later when Jesus redefines defilement (*koinóo*) as the evils that flow from the human heart rather than "disqualified from public rituals." Jesus restores her. The Septuagint uses *katharízo*, "to cleanse," to signify freedom from transgressions, return to God from rebellion and idolatry, and restoration of persons to both God and community *by the divine gifts of Spirit and the creation of new hearts*. Being *katharízo* through the healing of Jesus, she is healed, restored, and freed from whatever drives her—including perhaps rebellious idolatry:

> Have mercy on me, O God, according to your steadfast love; according to your abundant mercy blot out my transgressions. Wash me thoroughly from my iniquity, *and*

cleanse me from my sin. Hide your face from my sins, and blot out all my iniquities. *Create in me a clean heart,* O God, and put a new and right spirit within me.
🕮 PSALM 51:1–2, 9–10

I will cleanse them from all the guilt of their sin against me, and I will forgive all the guilt of their sin and rebellion against me. 🕮 JEREMIAH 33:8

I will sprinkle clean water upon you, *and you shall be clean from all your uncleannesses, and from all your idols I will cleanse you.* A new heart I will give you, and a new spirit I will put within you; and I will remove from your body the heart of stone and give you a heart of flesh.
🕮 EZEKIEL 36:25–26

Our shame-based inner dramas effectively repel Jesus: "Stay away! Don't look at me!" Shame conceals our alienation, stony hearts, and rebellion. When we recognize shame perhaps we can surrender it to God and learn to welcome *katharízo*—his cleansing word.

The Withered Hand
Once again we find Jesus addressing those gathered in the synagogue. A man with a withered (*xērainō*) hand appears (3:1–6). He knows his situation. Others know it. This time, the atmosphere is fraught with danger since the Pharisees have been stalking and criticizing Jesus, hoping to discredit him and neutralize his influence. They are actively looking to catch Jesus healing someone on the Sabbath.

True to form, Jesus *restores* (*apokathístēmi*) the man's hand, challenging those watching him. What exactly was restored?

Mark uses *zeraío* or *xēraínō* in this passage. That particular word relates the act to other passages in Mark's gospel where the word is used to describe lack of depth of soil or the inability to bear fruit:

> Other seed fell on rocky ground, where it did not have much soil, and it sprang up quickly, since it had no depth of soil. And when the sun rose, it was scorched; *and since it had no root, it withered away (xēraínō)*...And these are the ones sown on rocky ground: when they hear the word, they immediately receive it with joy. But they have no root, and endure only for a while; then, when trouble or persecution arises on account of the word, immediately they fall away.
> 4:5–6, 16–17

> In the morning as they passed by, they saw the fig tree *withered away to its roots*. Then Peter remembered and said to him, "Rabbi, look! *The fig tree that you cursed has withered.*"
> 11:20–21

Uses in the Septuagint of *xēraínō* link the passage to the greater story of Israel: mortality, faithless shepherds, and idolatry:

> I am he who comforts you; why then are you afraid of a mere mortal who must die, a human being *who fades (xēraínō) like grass?* ISAIAH 51:12

> Oh, my worthless shepherd, who deserts the flock! May the sword strike his arm and his right eye! *Let his arm be completely withered*, his right eye utterly blinded!
> ZECHARIAH 11:17

> Look, all its devotees shall be put to shame; the artisans [*makers of idols*] too are merely human. Let them all assemble, let them stand up; they shall be terrified, they shall all be put to shame [*be withered*]. ISAIAH 44:11

Let us consider the scene from another angle and enter it contemplatively from our physical experience. Hold your hand suitably. What might the withered hand symbolize? The man in the synagogue is unable or unwilling to give, to reach out a hand—to offer friendship or peace; to commit; to reach across the aisle. His withered hand signifies the incapacity to do meaningful work in the world, to create beauty, to open whatever is shut. At the same time, it symbolizes inability or unwillingness to receive other persons, welcome communion or gifts. I picture a hand clenched in resentment, fear, and pain. Shame, emptiness, or unworthiness fuels this.

Hmmm. In this story, Jesus does not simply heal the hand; remember, he *restores* it! In another healing story, the word *apokathístēmi*, "to restore, return," is also used:

> And the man looked up and said, "I can see people, but they look like trees, walking." Then Jesus laid his hands on his eyes again; and he looked intently *and his sight was restored, and he saw everything clearly.* 8:24–25

Apropos of our theme, Mark uses this word to connect the restoration of sight *and* hand. Ultimately, Jesus' entire ministry is about restoration. He is the one who has come to bring the people back to God—to follow the Way of life. In the Septuagint, *apokathístēmi* is used to describe the restoration of God's people and their return from Exile.

> *[Elijah] will turn [restore] the hearts of parents to their children and the hearts of children to their parents,* so that I will not come and strike the land with a curse. ⸂ MALACHI 4:6

> I will set my eyes upon them for good, and *I will bring them back [restore] to this land.* I will build them up, and not tear them down; I will plant them, and not pluck them up.
> ⸂ JEREMIAH 24:6

What would it take for us to receive full restoration, to God and each other? What would it take for us to approach the Light, holding out our withered hands?

A Woman Hemorrhaging
Another person comes to Jesus well aware of her condition: a hemorrhaging woman. The Marcan choice of *haíma*, "blood," to describe her malady connects with Septuagint passages about uncleanness and exclusion (e.g., Leviticus 15:19). Since we've studied "uncleanness" sufficiently, let us instead investigate the symbolic overtones of this particular ailment. Consider that scientists and doctors have told us that bleeding in the brain may alter mental function, producing confusion, weakness, slurred speech, loss of vision. And that shortness of breath, lightheadedness, pain, and weakness are associated with bleeding in the abdominal area.[9]

Imagine twelve years of foggy thinking, chronic weakness, blindness, difficulty speaking, lightheadedness, and pain. What would it be like to feel spiritually drained all the time—desolate, perpetually despondent, never nourished, dispirited, hopeless, and demoralized? Such desperation!

---

9 Thanks to Benjamin Wedro, MD, FACEP, FAAEM, "Internal Bleeding," http://www.medicinenet.com/internal_bleeding/page3.htm

What could deplete her so? Unrelenting poverty, rejection, hopelessness, abandonment, effects of trauma, taxing relationships, persistent absence of God, lack of basic affirmation, living in a dangerous place, incapacity to be nourished, heavy emotional or physical burdens, chronic anxiety, compulsion to take on others' burdens imprudently, self-hatred, and so on. Nevertheless, despite her desperate depletion she recognizes her need clearly and approaches the Light.

She touches Jesus' garment and sees she is cured. Mark employs the word *iáomai*, "to cure, heal," rather than *sózo* as he does elsewhere. The Septuagint uses help us understand that *iáomai* connotes curing spiritual Alzheimer's and sorrow:

> But your children were not conquered even by the fangs of venomous serpents, for your mercy came to their help and healed them. To remind them of your oracles they were bitten, and then were quickly delivered, so that they would not fall into deep forgetfulness and become unresponsive to your kindness. For neither herb nor poultice cured them, *but it was your word, O Lord, that heals all people.*
> ◆ WISDOM OF SOLOMON 16:10–12

> The spirit of the Lord God is upon me, because the Lord has anointed me; he has sent me to bring good news to the oppressed, *to bind up [cure] the brokenhearted*, to proclaim liberty to the captives, and release to the prisoners.
> ◆ ISAIAH 61:1

So we look at the woman and we think beyond the physical healing to a comprehensive healing of body and spirit alike. What would it mean for each of us to receive this sort of healing? What could help us see our plight in the manner of Bartimaeus, and turn to Jesus with the willingness and boldness of the hemorrhaging woman?

A Deaf Man
Context, context, context. Jesus takes the scribes and Pharisees to task for accusing his disciples of eating with unwashed hands. He turns the tables, indicting them for abandoning divine commands and promoting human conventions for cleansing everything (7:1–23). Jesus tells them, "It is what comes out of a person that defiles…" Next, he heals the daughter of a Syrophoenician woman who, because of her nationality, was considered unclean (7:24–30). Then, some people bring him a deaf person with a speech impediment—she couldn't hear, *kofós*, or speak, *mogilálos*. She is a stand in for disciples, scribes, and Pharisees alike.

Mark's listeners would associate both *kofós* (deaf) and *mogilálos* (unable to speak) with the divine promise of return to exiles:

> Then the eyes of the blind shall be opened, *and the ears of the deaf unstopped*; then the lame shall leap like a deer, and *the tongue of the speechless sing for joy*. For waters shall break forth in the wilderness, and streams in the desert.
> ◁ ISAIAH 35:5–6

Might our experience of exile in any form hint at what they dealt with—abandonment; rejection on grounds of race, religion, or sexual orientation; exclusion of any kind; the aftermath of bullying or other ways in which we are pushed away from others and community?

Jesus says to her, "Be opened! (*dianoígo*)." Does he refer to ears and tongue, or heart and mind? Once again, we consider the passages in the Septuagint that this word echoes:

Then the eyes of both were opened, and they knew that they were naked; and they sewed fig leaves together and made loincloths for themselves. GENESIS 3:7

On that day a fountain shall be opened for the house of David and the inhabitants of Jerusalem, to cleanse them from sin and impurity. ZECHARIAH 13:1

May he open your heart to his law and his commandments, and may he bring peace. May he hear your prayers and be reconciled to you, and may he not forsake you in time of evil. 2 MACCABEES 1:4–5

Indeed. *Dianoígo* draws contrasting meanings to itself—realizing personal, existential nakedness; life-cleansing water and an open heart. Realization of nakedness elicited shame in Adam and Eve; Jesus' words bring freedom to the deaf-mute burdened with shame.

Many of us have heard that pointed, and I believe accurate, observation, that "hurt people hurt people." In so many of these gospel stories, those who know weakness, alienation, and vulnerability stand in stark contrast to scribes, Pharisees, and disciples. Those who are injured, unhealthy, or in any way less than whole realize their need. Some ask for help. Some reach out and grab for health. Either way, they receive healing. Yet others react to Jesus intruding on their turf with pique, followed by shame and blame, hostility, threats, betrayal, and murder.

What appears to differentiate those who are able to embrace healing and those who cannot recognize Jesus as the source of healing is the knowledge of being overlooked and outcast. Those who recognize their humiliation are open to the miracle.

It is only when Peter sees how he denies Jesus that he comes to see himself in the same light as the leper, the blind, the deaf, and the possessed. Seeing the source of healing clearly, Peter turns and weeps and finds the *Way to Life*.

Segue

The discipline of prayer and reflection I will propose next intends to hold together the uncompromising and honest soul-searching asked of Jesus' followers with kind compassion and acceptance. Rigor by itself wounds. Kindness alone becomes squishy. We come to greater awareness of our life-setting by welcoming, in the context of acceptance, our patterns of resistance and blindness exposed. And we bring it all to the Light as best we can.

The final chapter describes some new and unexpected Best Friends Forever to help us lean in toward the Light.

QUESTIONS TO BRING TO YOUR PRAYER

1. An unclean spirit wonders, "What is God's plan for my life?" When Jesus appears, it cries out, "Have you come to destroy us!"
   - How do you relate "losing one's life and finding life"?
   - What does "dying to self" look like?
   - What in you welcomes and what opposes Jesus' mission?

2. Another unclean spirit seeks isolation. It wants to avoid being seen and confronted. A leper must warn others of her defect: "Stay away! Don't come near!"
   - Have you wanted to hide out from God, others, or yourself?
   - Have you pushed others away so your inadequacies don't show?
   - What might idolatry have to do with "not being enough" or "not good enough"? Might it have to do with shame? What has been your experience?

3. Hold your hand like someone with a withered hand.
   - What could that symbolize for you in your life?
   - What effects might that have on your sense of self?
   - How would "returning home from exile" mean restoration for you?

4. What depletes your physical, mental, or spiritual energy?
   - How does it affect the way you act toward others?
   - How would a cure bring you "good news to the oppressed, liberty to captives, and release to prisoners"?
   - How would it affect the way you treat others?

5. As we age, many of us become hard of hearing. Others deal with that in their youth.
   - What would it mean to you to really hear Jesus' teaching?
   - What blocks hearing the Word today?

Epilogue

GOOD NEWS FOR THE WAY

Guide me, my friends, to the pool of Siloam
Where the living Fountain flows.
Ease me down in the pool of Siloam
To wash the dreadful pain from my soul.
— ROC O'CONNOR, SJ, "POOL OF SILOAM"
(unpublished)

We have studied the story of Bartimaeus in the gospel context of Jesus' call to repentance, the gift to all that is epitomized by the words "You are my Beloved!" And we have seen how this blind beggar sitting at the crossroads between the *Path to Life* and the *Path toward Death* serves as a paradigm for contemporary discipleship. The log in our eyes, our daily dramas, and our well-protected comfort zones all declare our lack of sight, even as they hinder us from recognizing our personal and corporate plight. Will we ask to see? See what? See whom?

Sitting at this crossroads with our hearts broken open, we get to see Jesus more clearly. We also get to see with greater clarity our resistance to his teaching, his mission, and his destiny. First-world disciples can learn to associate personal experiences of alienation with the leper, the man with the withered hand, the dispirited woman drained hopeless and despairing, the one with the unclean spirits who kept hurting himself, and the person deaf and mute from rejection and abandonment.

Once we recognize that we are just like them, we may connect in a real way with others who struggle similarly. We might begin to see how the pain we avoid and suppress comes out as defensive aggression toward others who remind us of our woundedness. We may see how the very people we avoid in this life, much less the *stuff* in our lives we avoid, can become a place of deeper encounter with Christ. Here in this place of clarity and surrender, we begin to find, accept, and learn to encounter the Lord.

Seeing our situation clearly, we can, like Bartimaeus, beg to look up, to follow Jesus on the *Path to Life*, and be restored.

A Remedy

For we know
it belongs to your boundless glory
that you came to the aid
of mortal beings
with your divinity
and even fashioned for us
a remedy out of mortality itself,
that the cause of our downfall
might become the means of our salvation

through Christ our Lord…
- **Preface for Sundays III**

The church proclaims in this remarkable preface to the Eucharistic Prayer that temptations, wounds, resistance, and sins can become vehicles for salvation. Indeed, the good news is that the very "stuff" we assiduously avoid in ourselves and others can become a remedy for mortality. Oh, happy fault! O necessary sin of Adam! Not only is the light at the end of the tunnel the risen Christ, but the entire birth canal is filled with the Spirit of God. Let's delve into this good news. How might what we judge as our deficits become our new Best Friends Forever (BFFs)?

Prevenient Love
God loves us before we can respond to or earn divine love. Literally, grace "arrives before" (*prevenire*) we have any ability to construct our false but beguiling view of meriting this love. Prevenient grace stands in stark contrast to our habitual belief that we can make ourselves worthy: Can God love us more even if we were to become perfect? Not so much. Infant baptism illustrates this eloquently:

> Baptism, which is necessary for salvation, is the sign and the means of God's *prevenient love*, which frees us from original sin and communicates to us a share in divine life…[10]

Learning to inhabit the dissonance between God's prevenient love ("You are my Beloved!") and our need to win approval or stature ("Try harder. God will love me more when I…") can jumpstart the adult spiritual journey. That is, sitting with the fear

---
10 Congregation for the Doctrine of the Faith, "Instruction on Infant Baptism," no. 28.

of being small, abandoned, inferior, and rejected *while attending to* Jesus' good news locates us at the crossroads where we belong.

Justified by Faith—Redux

Christian theology calls the restoration of our wounded, sinful selves "justification." Some view this mainly through the lens of law and punishment: Human beings are fundamentally estranged from God because Adam's sin ruptured the relationship. God sent his Son to pay the price for human sin by dying a cruel death on the cross. The only way for humans to be saved from corruption and exile, then, is to acknowledge Jesus as personal savior and be "covered by the blood of the Lamb." You may be familiar with this interpretation.

On the one hand, I find this viewpoint helpful in its explicit sense of urgency. Repent! Now! It differs from other contemporary notions of spirituality that advance a rather vague notion of process. On the other hand, I don't appreciate its corollaries: the world is bereft of the presence of God; one-profession-of-faith-covers-all; lack of spiritual practices for growth and discernment over time; a susceptibility to "wash the outside of the cup" and not go within; and the blind eye to shame that this portrayal promotes. It asks us to believe that sinners remain depraved, guilty, corrupt, and alienated even while covered by the blood of the Lamb. The outside looks acceptable to a just God; inside is a steaming pile of…

In my experience, shame stymies introspection. "Can't go there." Therefore, instead of law-judgment-punishment as the lens through which to understand justification, I recommend transubstantiation. Surprise! St. Thomas Aquinas applied Aristotle's philosophy to the mysterious transformation of the bread and wine of the Eucharist into the Body and Blood of Christ. It speaks to the fact that their very substance, their "essence," is transformed through the grace of God. In the same way, I believe, God's grace works in the human person a slow, subtle, God-given, *total* conformity to Christ *with our collaboration*. Every part of us will be transformed into Christ. Perhaps a bit in this life.

Yes. It's a particularly Catholic point of view!

New BFF I—Creaturehood

All we are is dust in the wind.
🎵 "DUST IN THE WIND," KANSAS

It is sooooo easy to preach about being a creature of God. Yet it's so damnably inconvenient to live as vulnerable, precious creatures. I prefer grandiose dramas of heroic greatness or miserable dereliction. You? Who really wants the uncertainty and ordinariness of a mere creature? Let's build protective walls to defend against accident, chance, and change, all features of the life of a creature who does not have the power to control life or fate. Let's deny our vulnerability and tell ourselves that we're *the* exception—we have power!

Creaturehood names it all as dust in the wind. It whispers, "You live only for a brief time. You are not God. You are, in fact, never completely sufficient nor will ever have enough or be enough." "Silence! Give me self-sufficiency!" Rely totally on God all the time? "Nice idea, Jesus. Next! I know how to fill my emptiness, shore up my sense of inadequacy by myself!"

Yet, we walk with the Twelve who desire the same things—illusory glory, prestige, applause—until the very end. We remain dull and obtuse to Jesus' teaching about the last becoming first and the great serving everyone else. Until Peter's denial, he could not see and accept his fear and vulnerability. Tell me I'm wrong, but don't we hold at bay every profound encounter with Jesus lest we be changed?

Perhaps one day, like Francis of Assisi, we can learn to embrace the inner leper of our insufficiency and see our creaturehood as a blessing.

A New BFF II—Temptation

I was taught from my youth to avoid temptation—"the devil on one shoulder and an angel on the other." Well, win some; lose some. Not that I was lax about sin. I really tried. Being a good Irish Catholic boy, I lived every day saturated with shame and guilt, especially after puberty. Temptations 10,000 – Roc 3!

Not Jesus. In his first temptation in the desert, he does not fall prey to the most common human temptation—to make one good thing be something it isn't. Bread is not stone. Each is good in its own way. Jesus endures his all-too-human craving because he recognizes the difference! He isn't compelled to make something be what it isn't, because he embraces his precious and insufficient creaturehood.

Perhaps temptations, then, help us avoid our creaturehood. We were taught to flee temptations, to tighten the lid on them, and to feel shame when we fail. Doesn't work, does it? The harder we try to control the things that tempt us, the more they win. Our push-back creates even more resistance. But what if we're actually trying to repress our terror of vulnerability, which, in turn, activates our temptations?

Consider, instead, this approach—spiritual judo. Accept the brunt of temptation's attack, pivot, and send its force elsewhere. Instead of confronting temptation "manfully," surrender and ask for help: *"The cause of our downfall becomes the means…."* For example:

ONE: *Thank you, God, for this temptation.* I cannot control my inclinations to act out. I am your creature.

TWO: *I want to prove myself worthy by dealing with this temptation* ON MY OWN! I don't want to ask for help!

THREE: [Pivot] *Instead, I surrender it to you along with my "right" to be in charge.* (I don't like letting go!)

FOUR: *Please help me.*

When we surrender our frantic need to fill our emptiness, our deficits (avoiding creaturehood by controlling temptations) can become assets (admitting vulnerability). We stand before *Christ, well-situated as frail creatures of God*! Our friends in the "Twelve Step" community practice this every day; many of them have become masters of the sort of spiritual judo I've described. Seek them out!

New BFF III—Distractions & Expectations

I've come to believe that our attitudes about prayer are intimately connected to our expectations of what we want from prayer. I want prayers answered. I seek relief from fear, sorrow, temptations, or cares. I want freedom from all that so I can go on *my* merry way. That's what I expect. You? Well, in truth, our God is a sneaky god.

Grace lightens our burdens; it encourages and strengthens us. Consolations beguile us, summoning us to the garden in anticipation of sweet delights and nectar of the gods. We enter unguarded. We joyfully claim the garden as our own. We resolve to pray every day. Such comfort! Illumination! Joy! Healing!

If only it were like that all the time. Indeed, our God is a tricky god. Once we commit to pray, what happens? Eventually all the "stuff" we don't want to face surfaces. "I shouldn't feel angry, horny, hungry when I pray; I shouldn't be making lists. Take these away! Boring! Ugh. I must not be doing it right! I'm outta here." It's all this "stuff" that breeds distractions, the bane of everyone's prayer life. They scuttle our best intentions. Disappointed, we abandon our prayer project. Chalk up another failure. Why can't I do this right?

However, distractions can be our new BFF. Really.

Jesus befriended sinners, sent away unclean spirits, and healed those who knew they were deaf, dumb, and blind. He turned expectations on their heads—the last, first; the greatest, servants; the revered scribes, ravenous locusts. In Matthew and Luke, he castigates the Pharisees for not washing the *inside* of the cup! Why? It's the unseen matter on the inside of the cup that generates distractions.

Prayer is the crucible into which we slip, hoping for perpetual consolation. Yes, we are often blessed with peace when we pray. But very often we are beset by the never-ending rush of thoughts and feelings that distract us from being present in that moment to God. I propose that we can't be present to God if we are unwilling to be present to ourselves. Over the long haul, we cannot connect with God while disconnected from our primal, creaturely powerlessness, our dear and wounded selves.

But there is good news! Christ already dwells in these depths we compulsively avoid! All these rejected parts of life can lead us to encounter Christ *as we are at the crossroads*—lonely, empty, unworthy, insufficient, and afraid. They can become the means of our salvation. A hard truth: our dreams of greatness, applause, fullness, worth, adequacy, and adoration that pour forth from our deep longings merely weave together the scrim behind which we quail. It is so difficult to discover intimacy with God or anyone else as we continue to cover up our costly wounds of abandonment, shame for failing, or fear of being cast aside again. "Meet me as I am, O God."

I'm not saying it's easy, although it is pretty simple. Purification from pretense is so damn painful! We can choose as much restoration in this life as we can stand or stay with the ongoing pain of continually abandoning ourselves and taking that out on others. And so, just as with temptations, tracing the line back from distractions to unwanted feelings locates us in the crucible of prayer with Christ as we are. Thus, our new BFFs can teach us to become more present to the Presence.

The grace and mercy of God will transform everything in the next life—and perhaps thaw our frozen hearts in this life at least a bit as we take to heart:

> For I am convinced that neither death, nor life, nor angels, nor rulers, nor things present, nor things to come, nor powers, nor height, nor depth, *nor anything else in all creation*, will be able to separate us from the love of God in Christ Jesus our Lord. ROMANS 8:38–39

INTERMISSION 3: A STORY! A STORY!

The Feast of the Baptism of the Lord 2017. Noon Mass at the Church of the Gesu, Milwaukee. Around 140 of the faithful had gathered. The lector had just begun the First Reading (Isaiah 42:1–4, 6–7): "Here is my servant whom I uphold, my chosen one with whom I am pleased…" Three-year-old Joshua began wailing so loudly I couldn't hear the lector:

He shall bring forth justice to the nations, not crying out, not shouting, not making his voice heard in the street. A bruised reed he shall not break, and a smoldering wick he shall not quench, until he establishes justice on the earth; the coastlands will wait for his teaching…
◆❧ U.S. LECTIONARY VERSION

Ironic, eh? Joshua was adamant about being heard. His mom tried this and that and finally carried him to the back of the lower church in time for the beginning of the gospel.

I first addressed Jonah and Clare, Joshua's older siblings, to let them know I would say good things about their mom. "So, we just heard the Father proclaim, 'This is my beloved Son, in whom I am well pleased.' So, how many of you were upset at the little guy?" Hand-in-cookie-jar looks!

"There is irony here," I continued. "Jesus goes out to preach what he heard to a world crying out in pain: 'You are my beloved daughter, my beloved son.' And we wanted to gag the kid! Katie didn't berate him or batter him. She knew what to do." By now, I could see her in the hallway talking to him, holding him, soothing him. That's what moms do. And she calmed him in time to return for Communion.

Here's an analogy: For thirty-eight years, I've heard in confession how people beat the stuffing out of themselves to shape up. It hasn't worked. Otherwise, we'd have tons of "holy" people (read: *righteous* people) in the world. More and more, I believe that God in Christ through the Spirit labors long to speak to us, listen to us, hold us, soothe us.

Pope Francis addressed the Jesuits' General Congregation exhorting us to "pray for consolation" (see the Preface to the Eucharistic Prayer, quoted above) because that's what changes people. Threatening, trying harder, and strengthening our good intentions to change does not. It simply doesn't work! Why is it so difficult to imagine Christ saying to each of us, "You are my beloved daughter/son"? I suggested that after Mass, we could rightly thank Katie for being an image of God in our very midst. And for reminding us of how God deals with the inherent violence that lurks in our souls.

New BFF IV—Doubt
My longtime friend and colleague Dan Schutte once shared how doubt is *not* the opposite of faith. Rather, the opposite of faith is certainty. I agree with him. You and I construct defenses to defend us from worry, confusion, and disappointment. Allergic to anxiety, we treat doubt as the enemy and certainty as our champion. Whereas, often enough, doubt signals we're outgrowing the faith that previously kept us safe. Loss and disillusionment can pry us out of our comfort zones, right? We then get to choose to seek Christ more deeply or to invest more heavily in security systems. Either way, easy does it.

Tracing our uncertainty back to anxiety, and being willing to meet Christ anew *in* uncertainty, can prepare us for knowing and being known by him.

New BFF V—Grudges
Have you ever heard of "Irish Alzheimer's"? It's said that my people forget everything but the grudge. You? Resentment replays insults, wrongs, and hurts. It allows us to feel bigger and stronger rather than weak, small, and fearful. "You did this to me!" runs through our minds, again and again. Grudge-time. And over time, the other bears more and more responsibility while we take on less and less fault. It's a favorite script many of us use over and over. Scripts usually skip over the part where the resentful person plots revenge from fear of fragility.

Killjoy alert!

Justifiable anger cannot be justified. Contemporary action movies identify heroism with vengeance. Having had his vulnerability displayed for all to see, the hero takes up the right to kill. He says, "I've had enough. I'm now entitled to beat my enemy to a pulp and then kill him. And walk away laughing. Ha ha!" Justified anger is a ruse to avoid vulnerability for persons absolutely petrified of feeling small.

Recall how ten of the Twelve began a grudge match against James and John because they sought to outmaneuver them to be number one. I'm sure it was a grand dust-up that day!

Here's how I was taught to pray with my grudges (many times a day!):

> ONE: *God bless (whomever).* You know what he/she needs to be fully alive and joyful in you. Bless him/her with that grace.
>
> TWO: *God help me* with the grace I need to be fully alive and joyful in you.

Try it. It may make your grudges doors to the divine.

New BFF VI—Compulsions

Over the past thirty-eight years that I've celebrated the sacrament of reconciliation with people, many penitents have confessed persistent struggles with anger and lust. Temptations prompt the person to act out compulsively even in the face of repeated vows to control their actions. How can such compulsions become BFFs and turn us back to God?

First, I regularly recommend the person seek a trusted confessor, spiritual director, therapist, or twelve-step group. There is nothing quite as powerful as walking with a companion on the journey of healing. Problem is, most of us prefer to go it alone, impelled by shame and remorse.

Second thought: We respond in anger (gossip, impatience, grudges, rage, violence) to threats to our security, prestige, relationships, or self-will. It's a defensive action. We inflate ourselves to avoid feeling weak, impotent, or fearful. That is, we protect our precious vulnerability and creaturehood. In a similar way, we act out sexually to comfort ourselves from these and other unwelcome emotions.

Whether dealing with anger or lust, consider how our dear yet terrible emptiness or unworthiness fuels our compulsions and impels us to act out. One significant action we can take is to bring *all* of our lives into the crucible of prayer within which we encounter Christ-already-present. And bring what we discover into the light with confessor, therapist, or twelve-step group. The healing awaits, if like the man in the synagogue, we are willing to extend our withered hand.

New BFF VII—Prayer Redux

The beloved Prayer of St. Francis situates us as servants of Christ's mission. Show us where hatred, injury, doubt, despair, darkness, and sadness abide. Send us to sow love, pardon, faith, hope, light, and joy. We need this prayer more than ever to inspire us to act on behalf of the vulnerable and alienated. And to act on behalf of those whom we crucify every day because we avoid our own vulnerability and alienation. Hurt people hurt people.

Here's a thought: What if we prayed *this* way also? Enter the crucible and allow Christ to pray it for us, with us, and in us. Receiving his prayer for our healing may lead us to compassionate acceptance of our weaknesses and the weakness of others. Perhaps one day we may see through Christ's eyes, not just through the log in our own eyes. And perhaps the prayer might help thaw our frozen hearts, even just a bit.

Make me an instrument of your peace.
Where there is hatred, let me sow love.
Where there is injury, pardon.
Where there is doubt, faith.

Where there is despair, hope.
Where there is darkness, light.
Where there is sadness, joy…

Conclusion

More and more I am coming to believe what the church proclaims in the Preface I quoted earlier: "You…fashioned for us a remedy out of mortality itself, that the cause of our downfall might become the means of our salvation." There is *nothing* in our lives that God cannot use as a means of salvation. Bartimaeus is an iconic example of that truth, and his journey—self-awareness, request, receiving, and following—can become the path each of us takes.

Openness to the healing grace of God involves honest self-reflection and recognizing that our repetitive patterns of acting out, say, in envy, pride, gluttony, lust, fear, and anger tell us *that* we are stuck. Our frustration at being stuck could tell us it's time to inquire within our compulsive patterns concerning what fuels them. And this might lead us to look at what's inside our own cup. Seeing with new eyes would reveal the cup as a crucible where Christ always dwells with us in our blindness, our distasteful creatureliness, and our bothersome poverty. At some point, we may become willing to enter the crucible of prayer.

Perhaps then, we may realize how we sit at the crossroads beside Bartimaeus, knowing our blindness and poverty. We may become willing to ask, to beg, to look up to see God's covenant fidelity revealed in Christ. We could discover our hearts thawing a bit. And walk behind him on the *way*, learning from his teaching. We may even see how our hands can reach out to others, our hells become purgatory, our superficiality uncover its depths, all leading us to become wounded healers.

Virgil led Dante into the hell of human woundedness, through purgation, to the brink of heaven. Only after such a harrowing exploration would Dante fully accept being "Beloved" and be received by his beloved Beatrice into the realm of Outpouring Love. Perhaps this points to our path today.

OF RELATED INTEREST

On Eagle's Wings
A Journey through Illness toward Healing
JAN MICHAEL JONCAS

About ten years ago, Fr. Michael Joncas contracted Guillain-Barré syndrome, a debilitating physical condition that left this enormously active teacher, musician, and liturgist weak and drained. The challenges and frustrations he experienced while on the road to recovery led to a time of deep spiritual insight. This book is the fruit of that discernment, offering five key spiritual insights to deepening one's relationship with God in times of darkness—leading at last to a more profound relationship with God and God's goodness.

128 PAGES | $14.95 | 5½" X 8½" | 9781627852159

Holy Wind, Holy Fire
Finding Your Vibrant Spirit through Scripture
PAMELA A. SMITH, SS.C.M.

How can we get to know and draw closer to this Third Person of the Holy Trinity, who has the power to transform us and give us a share in the very life of God? Sister Pamela invites us into a wonderful journey through the Old and New Testaments to catch glimpses of the Spirit at work. Reading, reflecting, and praying with this book will help to re-energize and reawaken us to the energy and joy that only the Holy Spirit can give.

136 PAGES | $14.95 | 5½" X 8½" | 9781627853170

A Deep, Abiding Love
Pondering Life's Depth with Julian of Norwich
JENNIFER LYNN CHRIST

Jennifer Christ draws parallels between Julian's times and ours and demonstrates how Julian's message of hope and joy in God's never-ending love for us can give us strength and hope. Scholars have called Julian a theological optimist. Spend time with this book—reading Julian's words, praying with them, pondering, and journaling, and letting her hope-filled message take root in your heart.

128 PAGES | $14.95 | 5½" X 8½" | 9781627853156

TO ORDER CALL 1-800-321-0411
OR VISIT WWW.TWENTYTHIRDPUBLICATIONS.COM

TWENTY-THIRD PUBLICATIONS
A division of Bayard, Inc.